A CONSTRAINTS-LED APPROACH TO GOLF COACHING

While the popularity of golf is coming under increased pressure, it continues to hook millions of players. However, the complexity of the game and the extremely high level of precision required to hit the ball consistently well means that it is a game that is difficult to even become 'good' at, let alone master. Consequently, irrespective of whether the player is a weekend golfer, a club member, or a tour professional, the search for the key to playing good golf feeds an insatiable desire for ideas and tips to improve golf performance and bring one's handicap down. However, traditional coaching, with its primary focus on developing the perfect swing is not leading to a reduction in handicaps and the time is ripe for a new approach. This book aims to fill this void and is a landmark text for golf coaches and players about applying a constraints-led approach (CLA) to golf coaching. In this book, two golf coaches, Pete Arnott and Graeme McDowall talk to Ian Renshaw to demonstrate how their practice is driven and inspired by their alignment to a CLA. *A Constraints-Led Approach to Golf Coaching* includes case studies and examples of how constraints are manipulated to induce adaption in the technical, tactical (or put in golf terms, course management), physiological, and psychological development mechanisms needed to improve at golf. Examples cover coaching from their work with beginners, high handicappers, aspirant tour players, and elite players looking to make the 'tour'.

Ian Renshaw is an Associate Professor at the Queensland University of Technology, Brisbane, Australia. Ian co-authored the Foundation text in this book series (Renshaw, I., Davids, K. D., Roberts, W. & Newcombe, D. (2019). *Sport coaching, training and performance: Principles of constraints-based practice*. London: Routledge) and is also a series editor. Ian's teaching and research interests are centred on applications of ecological dynamics to sport settings. Ian has worked with numerous elite sports teams and national bodies providing coach education and skill acquisition consultations. In his spare time, Ian lives on the golf course.

Peter Arnott is a Golf Coach based in Edinburgh, Scotland. Peter obtained his Master's degree in Science Research in 2019. His thesis involved interviewing 7 European Tour players on their experience of preparing for, and then playing on the European Tour. He has also presented at the English Institute of Sport, World Scientific Golf Conference in St Andrews, Scotland, and to the Rio Olympics 2016 Gold-winning U.K. Women's field hockey team on effective practice and technique change. As a professional coach, Pete has worked with players of all ability levels from European Tour Players, Mini-Tour Players, competitive youth golfers, elite amateurs, and recreational players alike.

Graeme McDowall received an MPhil in Sports Coaching (Education) from the University of Birmingham, UK. He is a Lecturer in Golf and Sport at Scotland's Rural College (The SRUC) and a member of the Professional Golfers Association of Great Britain and Ireland. His main area of interest is skill acquisition in sport and as well as being a practitioner in this area with the high-performance golf programme at the SRUC, Graeme has delivered numerous skill acquisition presentations at key industry events and has shared his knowledge of this area with many of the world's leading golf coaches.

Routledge Studies in Constraints–Based Methodologies in Sport

Series Editors: Ian Renshaw, Queensland University of Technology, Australia
Keith Davids, Sheffield Hallam University, UK
Daniel Newcombe, Oxford Brookes University, UK
Will Roberts, University of Gloucestershire, UK

A constraints-led framework has informed the way that many sport scientists seek to understand performance, learning design, and the development of expertise and talent in sport, but its translation from theory to everyday coaching practice has proven challenging. *Routledge Studies in Constraints-Based Methodologies in Sport* provides practitioners and academics with material relating to the full breadth of the application of a constraints-based methodology in sport to in order to bridge this gap.

Introduced by a foundational text which sets out a practical design framework, and including concise books on sport-specific studies written by expert coaches, the series includes content on motor learning, skill acquisition and talent development for undergraduate and postgraduate students, and specialist knowledge on different constraints-led models for coaches, physical education teachers, sport scientists, and performance analysts.

The series provides the most comprehensive, theoretically sound, and practically relevant guide to understanding and implementing constraints-led approaches to skill acquisition and talent development.

The Constraints-Led Approach
Principles for Sports Coaching and Practice Design
Ian Renshaw, Keith Davids, Daniel Newcombe, and Will Roberts

A Constraints-Led Approach to Golf Coaching
Ian Renshaw, Peter Arnott, and Graeme McDowall

A CONSTRAINTS-LED APPROACH TO GOLF COACHING

Ian Renshaw, Peter Arnott, and Graeme McDowall

Routledge
Taylor & Francis Group

NEW YORK AND LONDON

First published 2021
by Routledge
52 Vanderbilt Avenue, New York, NY 10017

and by Routledge
2 Park Square, Milton Park, Abingdon, Oxon, OX14 4RN

Routledge is an imprint of the Taylor & Francis Group, an informa business

© 2021 Taylor & Francis

The right of Ian Renshaw, Peter Arnott, and Graeme McDowall to
be identified as authors of this work has been asserted by them in
accordance with sections 77 and 78 of the Copyright, Designs and
Patents Act 1988.

Library of Congress Cataloging-in-Publication Data
A catalog record has been requested for this book

ISBN: 978-0-367-48268-8 (hbk)
ISBN: 978-0-367-48267-1 (pbk)
ISBN: 978-1-003-03891-7 (ebk)

Typeset in Bembo
by codeMantra

Peter Arnott

None of my contributions would have been possible without my awesome wife, Shelley. Thank you, Shelley, from reading, then listening to my garbled ramblings, to keeping the two rugrats out of my hair.

To Johan & Juliet, for their constant loving interruptions to play or ask questions.

To my Family, Bob, Pauline, Michael, Lennon, Mike, Frances, Mags, David, Anne, David, Uncle Alec, Aunt Moira, and Aunt Helen, you're all a little bit unstable. However, if you read this book a little bit of instability is fabulous for one's growth and development!

In memory of Mum and Dad.

Ian Renshaw

I dedicate this book to the memory of my dad, Ernie.

To my wife, Alison, Hannah and Matthew, and my mum, thank you for your continued support.

Graeme McDowall

I dedicate this book to the continuing love and support of my wife Gillian, my children, Aiden and Carla, and my parents, James and Celia McDowall.

CONTENTS

FIGURES

TABLES

PREFACE

The game of Golf continues to hook millions of players. However, the complexity of the game and the extremely high level of precision required to hit the ball consistently well, means that it is a game that is difficult to even become 'good' at, let alone master. Consequently, irrespective of whether the player is a weekend golfer, a club member, or a tour professional, the search for the key to playing good golf feeds an insatiable desire for ideas and tips to improve golf performance and bring one's handicap down. To that end, thousands of books have been penned and millions of words committed to the pages of golf magazines. Online resources are a more recent source of knowledge with literally thousands of instructional videos available on YouTube and other social media sites. The overwhelming majority of these articles and 'tips' have focused on mastering the technique and are often marketed as what Newell and Ranganathan (2010) describe as the *champions model*. In the search for success, golfers are sold the line that if they learn the putting, pitching, and driving 'techniques' utilised by world-class golfers they too will become a top golfer. Such headlines are often accompanied by suggestions of reduced playing handicaps even though advances in equipment technology are regarded as the reason for a slight reduction in playing handicaps in the last thirty years (*https://www.golfdigest.com/story/a-closer-look-at-handicap-data-shows-just-how-much-golfers-have-improved-in-recent-years*). The golf coaching literature is dominated by an obsession with technique, highlighting the shortcomings of traditional player development methods in golf. In reducing a golfer's performance to nothing more than technique, golf coaching fails to capture the true multiplicative, non-linear, and dynamic nature of the human system as it interacts with the unique and ever-changing environment of each individual golf course. One reason for this potential shortcoming is the absence of an accessible theoretical framework that can capture the key elements of both the learner and the learning processes that underpin golf performance. This book, which sits as part of a series of sports-specific books, aims to provide exemplars from practitioners whose coaching is underpinned by such a framework. Here, we look at the challenges associated with moving beyond the narrow focus on coaching swing mechanics through the eyes of two qualified golf coaches, Pete Arnott and Graeme McDowall, whose practice is driven and inspired by their alignment to the Constraint-Led Approach (CLA).

After an initial introductory chapter where we will introduce the key ideas of CLA from a golf perspective, the rest of the book will chronicle the experiences of Pete and Graeme and will include case studies and examples of how they design learning environments to induce adaption in the technical, tactical, (or put in golf terms, course management), physiological, and psychological development mechanisms needed to improve at golf. Examples will be drawn from their work with beginners, high handicappers, aspirant tour players, and elite players already on the 'tour'. Throughout the book, we will use "I (Initials)" to reflect that the stories are being told by one of the authors from their experiences or "we" if the point we are making is a collective one. It is worth noting that although we are all advocates and use a CLA in our work, we often interpret ideas and concepts in our own unique way. This is why we refer throughout to 'a' CLA rather than 'the' CLA.

Our Overall Aims in This Book Are To:

1   Create a landmark text for golf coaches and players in relation to applying a CLA to the player development process across the skill spectrum from the beginners to the elite;
2   Explain through practical examples the key guiding principles of a theoretical framework (ecological dynamics) that underpins a CLA. In doing so it is hoped that the book inspires a paradigm shift in thinking in relation to instruction and practice methodologies within golf;
3   Demonstrate how a CLA approach can be applied to individual or group coaching;
4   Outline the non-linear nature of performance development and demonstrate how a CLA is an appropriate framework with which to organise thinking within this situation;
5   Use case studies to provide real-world experiences and applications of CLA from players and coaches. Qualitative data will be shared from elite-level players in relation to the 'transfer of training to competition' and also demonstrate how 'successful' *Affective Learning Design*' (i.e., learning that captures and creates the emotions found when learning and playing) relies heavily on quality information in relation to the desired 'future' target performance context.

1

INTRODUCTION

Why We Need a New Way of Golf Coaching

Introduction

The scene, Sunday at the 83rd Masters, 2019; Tiger Woods, on the brink of one of the most incredible comebacks in golfing history is standing on the tee at the picturesque 153-yard Par 3, 12th. For very good reasons, Golden Bell (named to reflect the deciduous shrub that blooms around the hole), is the signature hole of the course and the second hole in the aptly named series of holes called Amen Corner. On any normal day, the hole is an intimidating one with Rae's Creek lying in wait for any under hit shot. Many Green Jacket dreams have sunk in the water at the 12th accompanied by groans from the crowd as the aspirant champion's ball 'plops' directly into the Creek or rolls back down the bank into the water. Some of the great names in golfing history had fallen victim to this most challenging of holes, including Arnold Palmer (1959), Jack Nicklaus (1964), Tom Weiskopf (1980), Larry Nelson (1984), Raymond Floyd (1992), infamously, Greg Norman (1996), Phil Mickelson (2009), Rory McIlroy (2011), and Jordan Spieth, 2016 https://www.golfdigest.com/gallery/masters-the-biggest-disasters-at-the-12th-hole).

On this day, the 12th threatened to be treacherous as play started early due to the threat of thunderstorms and predicted wind of 15–20 mph, with gusts to 25 mph, from the South-South East. Indeed, it proved to be a pivotal hole in the race to be champion as the tee shot required hitting into a gusting wind with the likely consequence of any miscalculation resulting in significant trouble. As Tiger was preparing to hit his shot, he was aware that a number of his rivals for the crown, Francesco Molinari, Brooks Koepka, and Ian Poulter had all finished in the water and dropped two shots. The commentators knew this was a pivotal moment in the tournament; how would Woods react? Would he manage to hold his swing together given the pressure on the shot? In fact, technique was the last thing on Woods' mind, he was more interested in collecting as much information from the environment as he could to help him construct a shot with the right level of force to hit his preferred landing spot on the green. We will let Woods take up the story from here:

> Well seeing guys ahead of me in the water, 2 guys playing with me and hit the water. Right now, at that moment it was Francesco's tournament, he's the one with a 2 shot lead...Well actually, Francesco hit first and then, we had noticed, Joe and I had noticed that Brooksie [Koepka] and Polts [Poulter] were both in the water, and I know from playing with Brooksie a lot that he's got a much stronger ball flight than I do, especially with the short irons. He just pierced through the wind. And for him to come up short, I'm sure he had hit a 9 Iron, I know he likes to hit that little hot bleeder of his...OK there might be something there. When I played that eleventh, eleventh hole over the trees, and I hooked that 7 Iron out there, I gave it a little bit more because of the wind coming off the left. I could see some of the water ripples; they were on eleven, before I was building my stance. I did one last look over and I could see the water ripples move a little bit more, and so I had to give a little bit more of a turn, which I did. Probably if I hit it a little past the flag as well, but I wanted to make sure I turned it. So, with that, I know it bounces around there in the corner, but, ehm, my whole game plan was to put it over the tongue of the bunker on 12. And seeing Francesco, I know he didn't hit it solid, but if he was trying to chip an 8, and chipping a flag 8, you know, it came up a little bit short. I was committed to hitting it on my spot, I just happened to draw it up against wind a little bit more, I wanted to, so I thought it was going to probably be a six feet or eight feet past where it was, and basically just got it on the green, and so I said 'Oh, that's why both Brooksie and Polts hit it up short. There's more wind into, than there is across. Then Tony hit a good shot, you could see it just getting killed at the end, it stalled out, moved, actually it was a really good shot, hit flush, got to its peak and you could see it stall out a fraction or so, that's all it takes, and it ended up short in the water.
> (PGA Tour, 2019)

This account provided by Tiger in an interview with Golf TV (PGA Tour, 2019), demonstrates the messiness and complexity of high-performance golf and how highly attuned the expert golfer is to the dynamics of the performance environment and how experiential knowledge enables them to search for and use multiple information sources. In this instance, key sources of information used, included: (1) his ability to read the wind through observation of its effect on the water in the pond in front of the green, and (2) observing his opponents' actions as this enabled him to 'go to school' by comparing his own action capabilities in relation to what he saw from his opponents. Tiger used all of this information to attune his actions to just give 'it a little more…and basically just got it on the green.'

This seminal moment in the 2019 US Masters tournament, demonstrates that expertise is more about a tight fit between the individual and the performance environment rather than the common emphasis on the development of the 'perfect' swing. Of course, we are not trying to suggest that the quality of the swing isn't important. Rather, reproducing the 'perfect' swing would not have been enough on its own without Tiger's ability to exploit the available information in the environment to calibrate his swing to (almost) perfectly match the conditions.

For coaches and players, reframing their skill acquisition goals away from the traditional goal of producing a repeatable, perfect swing, to one of enhancing the ability to pick up and exploit key information from the environment means a significant change in approach. In writing this book, we hope to provide you with a framework to support this new way of thinking. In this chapter, we will first consider current golf coaching practice and ask, why, despite the thousands of books and millions of words on the same subject in golf magazines written about player improvement, and the increasing number of instructional videos available on the internet purporting to give golfers the secret to lower scores, playing handicaps have hardly changed over the last 30 years. One might argue that trying to learn second hand from a book or watching a video is perhaps not the best strategy and money would be much better spent on some lessons with a golf professional. As two of the writers of this book are golf professionals, you might say we would write that, wouldn't we? However, without deriding our colleagues, we would also point out that the environment in which most coaches are required to attempt to work their magic is limiting their capacity to facilitate improvement. Essentially, we believe that the transfer of skills learnt in practice is limited because most golf coaching takes place away from the course, in environments such as featureless practice grounds, or driving ranges, or putting greens that are highly unrepresentative of the golf course (see Figure 1.1). These environments shape the way that coaches interact with players. By that, we mean that given the coach cannot see how a player *plays in performance*, the focus becomes on the golfer's technique, or essentially coaching becomes solely focused on improving the golf swing.

To that end, the 'techniques' utilised by world-class golfers in areas such as putting, pitching, and driving are seen as the 'nirvana' for the average golfer. Newell and Ranganathan (2010) have described these techniques as the *champions model* and the technical obsession that currently dominates golf coaching highlights the shortcomings of traditional player development strategies in golf. However, golf analytics reveal that there is no rigid 'one size fits all' approach to achieve success, emphasising the individual nature of performance and the need to consider that more deeply when coaching. For any golfer, Rory McIlroy should not try to work on the same exact parts of the game as Jordan Spieth and neither of them should try to work on the same exact parts of the game as Luke Donald. The same advice would obviously apply to all golfers regardless of handicap and coaches need to match their coaching to the specific fit between each individual and the environment.

FIGURE 1.1   The majority of golf practice and coaching takes place on featureless practice grounds and invite coaches to focus on swing technique.

In reducing a golfer to no more than the sum of the parts of their technique, these coaching models fail to capture the true multiplicative, non-linear, and dynamic nature of the human system. One reason for this potential shortcoming is the absence of an accessible theoretical framework that is able to capture the key elements of both the individual learner and the learning process. Before we go into specifics and introduce the Constraint-Led Approach (CLA), providing examples to bring the ideas and concepts to life, we will first pause to consider what we mean by skill.

A New Definition of Golf Skill

Given that our focus of this book is on skill adaptability rather than skill acquisition in golf, it would seem appropriate to define what we mean by skill (and adaptability). At its simplest, an avid golf fan might say that a highly skilled golfer is someone who consistently achieves the desired outcome of hitting the ball accurately with a 'sound' repeatable swing. Despite motor learning researchers long knowing that it is impossible to ever repeat a movement exactly (actually since the studies of Nikolai Bernstein in the 1930s), this viewpoint has prevailed in golf coaching and, as mentioned above, has seen the pursuit of a perfect golf swing as its main focus. In this view of skill acquisition, learning to hit a golf ball is, therefore, about acquiring programs in the brain that can then be recalled and run off like a computer program, or like reading a score when playing music.

Colloquially, this has been termed *muscle memory* by many people. However, we would point out that muscles don't have brains and theories of brain enrichment have largely been discredited for lack of evidence in the skill acquisition literature (see Renshaw et al., 2019). However, these ideas are strongly embedded in coaching practice across many sports and underpin the most common practice methods for developing accurate and consistent actions in specific performance domains (Araújo & Davids, 2011).

Golf practice that attempts to achieve repeatable swings, is, therefore, aimed at strengthening motor programs or schemas that can be 'run-off' as required (Schmidt & Lee, 2013) and has led to practice approaches where tasks are broken down into constituent motor programs before being 'added' back together (i.e., task decomposition, or what is commonly known as part-whole learning). In golf coaching, this type of practice is often seen when coaches ask players to swing the club by only practising one part of the swing or to reproduce a whole swing without a ball being present. Despite the popularity of such approaches in golf and sports coaching in general, decomposing practice tasks is supported by little actual research evidence. Essentially, research has failed to show that when movements are practiced by being pulled apart, they do not replicate those seen when performed whole.

In contrast, proponents of a CLA take a different view, proposing that skill should be framed as the *adaptation* or *attunement* of the individual to a performance environment (Araújo & Davids, 2011) rather than acquiring an internal representation of the movement. Coaching to support skill learning is, therefore, more about facilitating the emergence of an a*daptive, functional relationship* between a performer and his or her environment (Araújo & Davids, 2011). Essentially, this approach means that coaches should focus on helping players develop solutions that work (they are functional) by providing opportunities to become more and more 'adapted', or 'attuned' to the environments in which they play. Therefore, changing the working definition of skill that coaches use, means that the focus of golf practice moves away from the pursuit of the perfect golf swing to one which facilitates the emergence of greater functional relationships between the learner and the performance environment. With this new definition, a golfer becomes more skilled as the *fit* between their capabilities and the key features of the performance environment becomes tighter and tighter. Another way of looking at this is to consider Darwin's ideas of evolution. The organism that is best adapted to the environment survives and thrives as it learns to exploit available resources, while those animals that are not able to adapt do not survive. Likewise, the best golfers are the ones who learn to best adapt to their performance habitats and, therefore, achieve the best scores (survive) and ultimately, play in higher standard competitions (thrive).

When learning is about becoming better adapted to the performance environment, the focus of coaching switches to creating practice tasks that support players in developing the capabilities to solve the problems that the golf course and surrounding weather systems throw at them. Tiger Woods recollections from Augusta above highlights this point very well. Consequently, rather than attempting to create an 'idealised' repeatable swing, practice is about ensuring that each and every golf shot fits the demands of a specific performance situation. Put simply, this approach is about developing individual golfers, rather than golf swings. Helping players achieve this goal means more practice time needs to be spent 'simulating' playing golf *on the course*, rather than the typical golfers' practice session of hitting a bucket of 100 balls from the same spot, often with the same club on a featureless driving range. Coaching *on* the course provides the golfer with opportunities to attune his/her actions to the key information sources that immediately act as invitations for action in the environment (see later for a more in-depth explanation of key information sources which collectively provide *affordances*) to develop a range of functional golf shots (see Figure 1.2). Such coaching is focused on giving golfers the time and space to search, explore, and ultimately exploit key features of performance environments to facilitate stable yet adaptable movement solutions (Chow et al., 2015).

The impact of this new definition of skill learning has significant implications for the way coaches should work with individual players. A key requirement is that the performance context of each golfer is taken into account when constructing

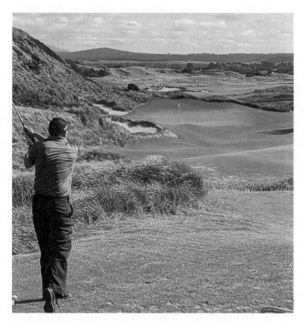

FIGURE 1.2 The affordances of the environment shapes a player's swing to create a ball flight that fits the environment. Here, on the 201 m Par 3 5th Hole at Barnbougle Dunes, Tasmania, the sunken nature of the green invites the golfer who has a natural draw to start the ball out to the right and use the natural contours to run the ball down onto the green. In contrast, the player who naturally fades the ball can look to land the ball on the bank in front of the green behind the bunkers on the left and let the ball run out to the pin. Of course, club selection is strongly influenced by wind velocity.

player development plans. For example, the requirements of the club golfer who only needs to become good on one course are different to the club representative player (i.e., pennant player in Australia) who needs to be able to adapt to a range of local courses, and the tour player who needs to be able to adapt to a much wider range of courses across a continent, or even the world. The club coach would, therefore, only need to design learning activities that help adaptation to the specific constraints of that course, whereas, the coach of a tour player would need to help the player adapt to a range of courses with a range of challenges. We will specifically focus on coaching the beginner and typical club golfer in Chapters 2 and 3, and the aspirant and actual tour player in Chapters 4 and 5. First, though, we will provide a broad outline of a CLA to golf coaching to enable you to put a CLA into action. Our first focus will be on demonstrating how the interwoven relationship between the individual and the environment is crucial to, (1) understanding a golfer's performance, (2), designing individual golf practice, and (3), implementing longer-term talent development programmes. We should point out that we will not discuss the theory that underpins CLA, and the interested reader is directed to the Foundation book in this series (Renshaw et al., 2019) and the earlier books (Davids et al., 2008; Chow et al., 2015) if interested to learn more.

The Individual-Environment as One System

As we have highlighted above, our new way of considering skill has important implications for golf coaches who need to design learning activities that support the emergence of the specific abilities (i.e., technical, course management, mental, emotional, perceptual, and physical) needed to succeed in the specific performance environments of the players we are coaching. Perhaps, understandably, coaching has focused on the individual without considering the impact that the environments play in shaping the emergent skills. When skill learning fails to consider how each individual interacts with the environment, it can lead to practices that fail to represent the task to be achieved. For example, on a recent trip to the driving range, Ian observed a coach delivering a coaching lesson to beginner-level adults. The coach spent some time teaching the group to mimic 'hitting' the ball by swinging the club in response to an imaginary ball. Once they had 'got it' (i.e., produced a 'good' swing), the ball was brought into the practice. However, the expectation that the swing would transfer to efficient ball striking failed to occur, with the coach shocked to discover that the well-rehearsed swing patterns were not replicated when a ball actually required hitting. These task decomposed approaches that focus on developing a perfect technique are a strong focus of practitioners across many sports. For example, P.E. teachers spend most of their time (up to 78%) engaging in such teaching strategies (Curtner-Smith et al., 2001). However, the lack of transfer in such tasks to the 'real thing' (Renshaw and Moy, 2018) emphasises the importance of practitioners considering the individual *and* the environment when designing skill learning activities.

As you will be aware by now, in this book our premise is that the appropriate level of analysis to describe golf coaching is to consider the individual *and* the environment as one system, an inseparable pair where each term implies the other (Gibson, 1986). In golf, the idea of mutuality of the individual and environment is significant, as it highlights that the type of player someone becomes is determined by the environments that he/she learns in. Importantly, this includes physical *and* cultural environments.

A good example of how the physical environment can significantly impact the emergent skill is to consider the difference in golf swings on the range and on the course. At the higher levels of golf, players generally get good practice facilities and have an unlimited supply of good quality balls. Coaches and players would be forgiven for thinking that such practice would be highly valuable in terms of supporting the development of a solid golf swing. However, evidence from sport scientists supports our view that golf swings are specifically shaped by the environment in which they take place. In our own coaching, we often find when measuring with a Trackman device a disparity and a lack of transfer in the quantifiable data produced by Trackman from range to golf course. We have yet to find a player that can consistently duplicate their Trackman numbers from the range to the course, purely because the golf course offers up more opportunities for different actions and it poses more questions to the golfer than the range (different angles, boundaries, lies, wind, club, elevation).

These findings do not appear to be skill level specific. For example, Bull (2015) undertook a biomechanical analysis of 11 European Tour players on the range, on the course, and then back on the range. Findings revealed significant differences between range and course swings; however, similar movement patterns were found in both range sessions. I (PA) experienced a similar result when working with 'Bruce' who was a high handicapper who came to see me for a series of lessons. Due to weather conditions the first few sessions took place on the range. Bruce wanted to work on striking the ball better with his irons and, after watching him hit a few balls, I could see that the problem was that the low point of the swing was behind the ball. We used the Trackman device to provide feedback on the low point of each shot which told us where he was making contact in relation to the ground. Figure 1.3a shows that initially, Bruce was getting a reading of 2.6B, which meant that he was hitting the ground 2.6 inches before the ball. I explained to him that ideally, we want to see a low point after he had hit the ball, so I challenged him to try and change the number from a B(efore) to an A(fter). I supported Bruce's exploration by asking probing questions such as what happens to your low point if you put the ball further forward in your stance, or if you put more weight on your front or back foot. After a few sessions, Bruce began to hit the ball more consistently and this was reflected in a low point reading of 2.6 inches after the ball (Figure 1.3b). Once the weather picked up we continued our lessons out on the course. Much to our surprise, the improvement did not transfer. Now, Bruce was back to hitting the ground before the ball, in fact it was worse than before as he was now hitting the ground 4 inches before the

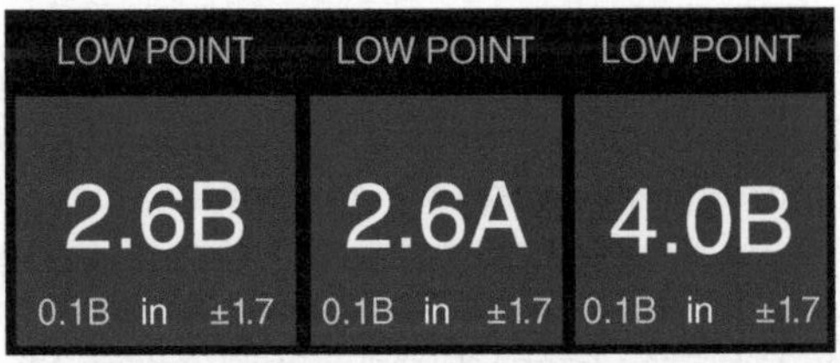

LOW POINT	LOW POINT	LOW POINT
2.6B	2.6A	4.0B
0.1B in ±1.7	0.1B in ±1.7	0.1B in ±1.7

FIGURE 1.3   Bruce's Low point scores on Trackman; (1) Pre-intervention on the range, (2) Post-intervention on the range, and (3) Post-intervention on the course.

ball (Figure 1.3c). I explained to Bruce that the various constraints that the golf course threw at him such as uphill, downhill, side hill lies, different grasses, and the wind were all factors that he had not had to deal with on the driving range and we needed to work on his low point on the course.

Pause for Thought 1: The Value of Measuring Golf Performance in the Lab

Indirect measures of performance from golf swings performed in laboratory conditions, indoors on simulators, or in featureless driving ranges may provide inadequate information about real golf performance due to the lack of representativeness of the performance environment (Keogh & Hume, 2012; Jenkins, 2014; Evans & Tuttle, 2015). These ideas can be thought about in terms of players who ask coaches to make judgements about their golf swings and the subsequent impact on club head velocity or ball flight characteristics. While these environments make it much easier to capture data from motion analysis systems as the environment can be made more controlled or standardised, their fidelity, that is, how closely the swings replicate those performed in actual competition on golf courses, is questionable. The effects of this are significant, as, when informational constraints are changed, there are significant changes in movement responses, decision-making, and performance outcomes. In golf, Bull's unpublished (2015) study comparing the golf swings of European Tour Players on the driving range and the golf course found significant differences in hand and arm movements between the two environments. These findings bring into question the value of learning to play golf on the driving range and an obvious question for the golfer brought up on the idea that you work on your swing on the range would be, why would the swing change? In essence, context significantly impacts a golfer's movements. For example, consider how the context of hitting a daunting 200 m shot into a headwind over water to make par and qualify for the cut in a tournament would potentially impact the emotions and thoughts of the player. As we know, changes in emotions lead to changes in perception (how we see the world), thoughts (how we are thinking about the world), and our actions (how we move). To verify the impact of these interacting factors on the golf swing for this shot would require the biomechanist to attempt to replicate the same conditions. Clearly, simply asking the golfer to hit a 200 m shot on the driving range without the context would be unlikely to work, even if the golfer was told to imagine hitting the same shot with the same consequence. In essence, the sport scientist would need to ensure that the 'experimental design' provided the key information present in the performance environment (i.e., the water and the consequences of failing) to ensure that the thoughts and emotions of the golfer were the same.

The importance of the cultural environment in providing the context in which a skill is learnt can be seen by the importance of the places where they grew up being reported as significant in the development of many golfing champions across the world (see Figure 1.4). To illustrate this point, we will consider how the childhood of Seve Ballesteros, one of the greatest golfers of all time, shaped his amazing creativity around the greens and enabled him to play some of the most breathtaking golf ever seen. Many have put the extraordinary imagination, delicacy of touch, and range of shots around the green that he possessed as a consequence of learning the fundamentals of the game with just one club – a 3 iron. "He was a

FIGURE 1.4 The history and culture of a golf club can have a significant impact on the emergence of young golfers. For example, the club's attitude to juniors practising and playing on the course can impact their likelihood of taking up golf and the skills they develop.

genius," said Tiger Woods on Seve's formal retirement from competitive golf in 2007, "probably the most creative player who's ever played the game" (Green, 2011). However, it was a confluence of factors that shaped his emergence as one of the greats, including the tradition of the area he grew up in producing great golfers, growing up in a golfing family with expert golfers 'on tap', and a limited range of clubs (one!) to practice with, and then, only sand to practice on (most of the time).

Pause for Thought 2: Where Did You Come From? Severiano Ballesteros

Seve was born on 9 April, 1957 in the small fisherman's village of Pedreña, in northern Spain. This area has one of the greatest golfing traditions in Continental Europe. Seve's brothers were golf professionals and his uncle, Ramón Sota, was one of the best players in Europe during the sixties. Significantly, Seve learnt to play golf using a wood-shafted 3 iron that his brother Manuel gave him, and developed a huge variety of shots playing *on the local beach* as he was not often allowed to play much on the local Royal Pedreña Golf Club unless he climbed over the wall in Pedreña to play the course on moonlit nights (https://seveballesteros.com/en/seve/biography/). Perhaps a hidden advantage that allowed (or forced?) him to spend most of his childhood practising golf was the fact that he was expelled from school at a very young age. His hard work was legendary and Seve himself reflected "between the ages of six and 23 I gave my whole life to golf" (https://www.golfdigest.com/story/).

A key feature of considering the mutuality of the individual and environment is that the individual is a perceiver *of* the environment and an actor *in* the environment. This captures the idea that what we see determines how we act, but that we also act to enhance what we see. As Gibson (1986) put it "we perceive to move and we move to perceive (p. 223)." For example, George, a scratch golfer told me a story that highlights the importance of searching to 'pick-up' information ahead of taking a shot. On a new hole at this home course that he had never played before, George told me that he had his second shot to a green hidden behind a steep bunker (see Figure 1.5). He pointed his range finder at the bunker and saw that it was 100 m, so he added 10 m onto the distance and decides to hit a high pitching wedge to just clear the bunker and land it softly on the 'middle' of the green. He hit the ball perfectly and walks up with a spring in his step and looking forward to a birdie putt. However, to his horror, when he walked passed the bunker, he found the ball in rough 25 yards from the front of the green, that was not situated as expected directly behind the bunker! His failure to walk up to the green and check its position,

FIGURE 1.5 Collecting as much information about any the environment and task requirements is a crucial part of any pre-shot routine. Failure to search for information can lead to misperceptions and subsequent mistakes. Here, on the new 4th Hole (350 m Par 4) at Nudgee Golf Course, Brisbane, the blind approach shot has led to many first-timers (like George) leaving their second shot short.

the pin position (and any slopes on the green), resulted in him misperceiving the distance he needed to hit the ball.

On a global level, the mutuality of the individual-environment emphasises that what we perceive (e.g., see, hear, feel, touch) in our environment guides what we do and how we act. What we perceive is dependent on what resources (i.e., driving ranges, putting greens, short game practice areas, golf courses, beaches) are available and then upon our ability to pick up the information that is offered by these environments. Perceiving is therefore about integrating relevant information from the different senses and is much more than just simply what can be seen, it is about hearing the sound of the wind, feeling it on your face, feeling the tightness of your grip on the club or the resistance of the club as you swing it through the rough on your practice swing, and the slope of a green from your adopted stance. All can provide you with valuable information to regulate performance, just like seeing ripples on the surface of the water did for Tiger in shaping his tee shot. This is a key concept for golf coaches as it highlights the importance of designing learning environments that provide players with opportunities to attune to information from the environment to which they can couple their actions. We discuss this key point by considering the following concept first.

Seeing the Golf Course through the Lens of Your Own Capabilities

When we consider how a golfer perceives a specific shot, we need to understand what it offers or invites for him/her (See Figure 1.6). For example, a straight 290 m hole offers an eagle opportunity for the golfer who can drive the ball 300 m, whereas, in contrast, a high handicapper who can only drive the ball 200 m will need to try to land his/her drive in an optimal position to play his or her second shot to attack the pin. Another example would be to consider how a golfer's action capabilities impact how they would read the break required on a specific putt. PGA Tour Putting coach, John Graham, recently described how different golfers might

FIGURE 1.6 How you see a particular shot is shaped by your action capabilities. What do you see here? The shot is 120 m into the green directly behind the tree on the right. Are you punching a shot under the overhanging branches, or hitting a high wedge/9 or 8 over the top? Or are you fading the ball around the tree if you are right-hander or drawing it if you are a lefty?

see the break on the same putt, such as a right to left sloping putt. The golfer who hits the majority of his/her putts straight (i.e., not pushing or pulling), would see a putt with 8 cm of break. However, another golfer who tends to pull his putts (left), would see a putt with a 10 cm break, while another golfer who tends to push his putts will see a 6 cm break. These examples highlight that every golfer will look at a course, a hole, and each shot on that hole in terms of what it offers or invites for them. This links to the concept of affordances which we will now introduce.

Affordances

Gibson (1986) proposed that the surroundings of the individual is his or her ecological 'niche' and is composed of a set or landscape of affordances for a particular animal (Chemero, 2003). Affordances consist of environmental properties that afford (provide) 'opportunities for action' for each individual. In fact, certain information sources in a performance environment may actually invite actions (Withagen et al., 2012, 2017). Affordances surround the individual's habitat; where he/she lives and is what it 'offers', and as highlighted in the previous section, consists of a range of resources that shape the range of emergent functional abilities that individuals can then exploit in their attempts to get a 'grip' of their environment. In learning situations, the environment offers possibilities or invites actions in the pursuit of goal-oriented abilities. Environmental features such as mediums (i.e., air, water in ponds, land), substances (i.e., course characteristics, trees, bunkers, mud, surfaces); objects such as the paraphernalia or tools of coaching (i.e., cones, markers, alignment poles); places (driving ranges, putting greens, short game area, par-3 courses) and events (lessons or tournaments), offer different possibilities for individual learners.

The theory of affordances is predicated on the idea that the environment consists of information that regulates the movements of individuals (Davids et al., 2008). In golf, this information would typically include environmental information such as the direction and strength of wind, the grain or incline on a green, or the position of hazards on the course. Whilst this information is always directly available for individual golfers and acts to constrain his/her actions (Gibson, 1986), the ability to use it is determined by the player's ability to actually 'pick it up'. This idea emphasises that for the golfer perceiving is an active process of searching for the key information that can be used to guide movements (see Figure 1.7). The reflections of Tiger at the beginning of the chapter capture this idea perfectly as he demonstrated his outstanding ability to gather as much information as possible before playing the shot on the 12th. Importantly for coaches, it is essential to understand that if they wish players to learn to pick up or 'attune' to the 'useful' information available in performance environments, that information must be designed-into experiences in the practice environment. The emergence of functional perception–action skills through practice is predicated on practitioners ensuring that key sources of information are present in practice environments and tasks. To emphasise this point, performers will only become attuned to specific affordances within practice and performance environments through continued exposure to them.

FIGURE 1.7 Picking up or 'attuning' to the key information on the green is essential for successful putting. Reading greens requires noticing the grain, contours and slopes, and hardness of the surface to judge pace. Understanding how the wind will affect the putt is another layer of complexity that needs to be factored in.

For the coach, this idea highlights the need to develop adaptable, intelligent golfers who 'know' what the environment offers them in relation to their own capabilities. For example, a ball sitting on a very hard, tight lie 5 m from the edge of a green, may be perceived as a great chipping opportunity for a player who is a very good chipper of the ball, whilst a player who is a poor chipper may see it as the ideal opportunity to putt. Coaching should, therefore, aim to increase players' ability to recognise and then exploit the landscape of affordances available on highly variable golf courses by providing players with opportunities to explore their action capabilities and develop a range of solutions. Hence, practice should be designed to require players to hit the ball off a variety of surfaces (i.e., hard, soft), with a variety of lies (i.e., uphill, downhill, below or above the feet), with a variety of grass types and lengths, with holes with different layouts requiring different ball flights matched to the demands of the course. Additionally, environmental conditions need to be taken into consideration. For example, wind conditions (head, cross) will impact the type of shot required (i.e., high, low,) and require the correct club selection. Hence, any golf learning environment must involve providing opportunities to learn to adapt to the huge range of environmental and task constraints that a golfer will face. Constraints are the boundaries that shape the emergent skills and are categorised as individual, environment, and task constraints. In the next section, we will provide a summary of what we mean by constraints and then provide a few examples of the key constraints in golf performance.

A CLA to Golf

Identifying the constraints (i.e., factors that act as boundaries that shape emotions, thoughts, perception, and actions) that potentially influence performance in sports is an important starting point for golf coaches (see Figure 1.8 and Table 1.1). Performer

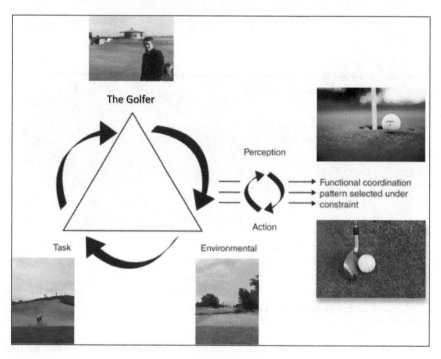

FIGURE 1.8 A Constraints–Led model of golf coaching.

TABLE 1.1 The constraints builder for golf

Individual	Environment	Task
Intentions	Wind	Course length
Height	Temperature	Scoring system
Limb length	Grass characteristics	Relative competition score
Weight	Course location	Competition position
Personality	Course contours	Clubs available
Skills: driving ability, iron play, short game, bunker play, putting	Weather conditions	Ball type
	Green speeds	Bunker characteristics
	Surface hardness	Sand type in bunkers
Fitness factors: strength, speed, power, flexibility, aerobic, anaerobic fitness, Fatigue	Club culture	Additional rules
	Opponents characteristics	Mulligans
	Atmosphere on the course	Speed golf
	Crowds	Other equipment
Muscular endurance	Match officials	–barriers, targets, guides
Mental factors: confidence, self-efficacy, emotional control, attentional control	Caddies	

constraints cover physique and mental skills such as self-confidence, emotional control and motivation, technical skills, and fitness levels, all of which can influence the way a golfer will approach a specific shot. Environmental constraints include physical environmental constraints such as weather conditions, practice facilities, and perhaps the layout of the local golf course that a player was raised on; cultural constraints such as family, peer groups, the culture of a golf club, and access to high-quality, developmentally appropriate coaching. Sociocultural historical constraints can have a powerful impact in influencing the way in which coaches design and organise practice activities. For example, the culture of golf may draw new coaches towards the adoption of traditional practice structures, performance habits, and customs of learning and development that fit with what golf coaching is thought to be about. A useful concept when considering sociocultural constraints is the idea that a community like that of golfers can be described as a 'form of life' (Wittgenstein, 1953, p. 15). A orm of life describes common ways of being (i.e., a golf coach) in terms of the normal behaviours and customs of specific communities" (Rietveld & Kiverstein, 2014, pp. 328–329). Within the context of the community of golf coaches, a form of life describes the values, beliefs, traditions, customs, and behaviours that influence attitudes towards the way we coach. Historical sociocultural constraints can be challenging when exploring new ideas in areas such as coaching and can often lead to negative responses especially from those individuals who have been successful in using a more traditional approach. This idea is captured in the response "well, it worked for me, didn't it." In response we would argue that many of the big shifts in performance levels across sport have emerged from an individual's ability to challenge the norms and try new ways. A great example here would be Dick Fosbury, who revolutionised high jumping by developing his 'flop' when his coach was not there.

Task constraints include the goal of the task, the rules of golf, equipment available, and the relative state of a tournament. Some of these constraints can be controlled by coaches, some can't. For example, individual constraints such as growth, height, maturation, environmental constraints, such as a change in wind direction, or the temperature, or task constraints such as a rule change imposed by a governing body or the opposition you play against in a competition, may all have an impact on the emergent performance but are outside the practitioner's control. Of course, just because these types of constraint cannot be controlled does not mean they should be ignored and practitioners can design-in opportunities to learn to explore and exploit such constraints. Other constraints such as strength, skill, nerves, the ability to read greens or know how the wind will impact ball flight, the lie of the ball, the distance to the flag, or the position of the ball in relation to hazards such as bunkers or water can be deliberately considered when designing practice tasks. Below is a summary of some of the most important constraints that coaches can choose from when building CLA sessions. We would point out that this list is not all-inclusive and the reader is encouraged to add their own.

Individual Constraints

While any one specific individual constraint can have an impact on performance, the most important individual constraint is one's *intention* (Kelso, 1995). In golf, intentionality is strongly related to picking up key information from the available affordances to inform decisions around the type of shot required in any situation and hence provide an overarching constraint to inform the selection of the most functional 'co-ordination pattern' that will best fit those intentions. Of course, a failure to pick-up key information in terms of what the available affordances invite or offer a player can lead to players setting inappropriate or badly framed intentions. Indeed, sometimes a lack of understanding of what the environment allows can lead to players setting intentions that are impossible to achieve. For example, a player new to golf came to us highly frustrated as he could not get enough height on his chips from around the greens at the new club he had joined. When we dug a little deeper into the problem, we figured out the problem and pointed out to him that on the very hard, tight lies he was hitting off, getting the ball high was not actually possible and that his intentions were not matched to the reality of the situation.

Kiverstein and Rietveld, (2015) introduced the idea of skilled intentionality which they defined as "the individual's selective openness and responsiveness to a rich landscape of affordances" (p. 701). This is the fundamental essence of decision-making in golf, which coaches can harness and develop in training designs. Because skilled performance can be framed in terms of a player's ability to attune and ultimately exploit the landscape of affordances, intentionality is a central constraint to be considered by practitioners and frames the selective openness and responsiveness of learners to search for and select from the rich landscape of available affordances (Rietveld & Kiverstein, 2014).

Another key point that needs to be considered when looking at a golfer's intentions is the fact that they act as a specific informational constraint that can influence whether a player tries to stabilise or destabilise existing movement patterns such as a signature golf swing. For example, a player may choose to stick with a current swing or attempt to completely remodel it after a few failures. Intentions are, therefore, very powerful and decisions to try and change well-established movement patterns can impact careers pathways. For example, one player we know who played on the European tour with a high level of success decided to completely change her technique after receiving advice from a new coach who based all of his advice on data collected on a Trackman. She had a functional technique; however, it was a little idiosyncratic and the coach's interpretation of the Trackman data told her that she was swinging with too much of a draw bias (right to left ball flight) and she needed to change her swing to get a straight ball flight. So, even though the incorrect numbers (according to the coach reading Trackman) resulted in her having a consistent ball flight, which she had hit all her life, they changed everything in an attempt to 'Zero out' her numbers on Trackman. Unfortunately, her performance regressed considerably and her career went rapidly downhill. Consequently, in golf, coaches need to be very aware of how intentionality can frame the way players interact with task and environmental constraints to facilitate changes between or refinement of different functional patterns of behaviour (Button et al., 2020).

Closely tied to intentions is an understanding of the goals of golfers so that coaches can design sessions to match their specific wants and needs. For example, performers are often resistant to attempts by coaches to change well-established techniques that have been somewhat successful. Consequently, attempts to change movement coordination by manipulating task constraints or providing augmented instructional constraints can be 'over-ridden' by individual intentional constraints (Kelso, 1995), and coaches need to convince their charges that a new performance approach is going to be better than well-established techniques. Often, it takes failure for this to happen and practitioners may sometimes manipulate constraints to deliberately create such an outcome. Of course, adopting such an approach can be a high-risk proposition and practitioners need to ensure that the right psychological support is provided at these times. A good example of this was a recent coaching session I (PA) undertook where a beginner asked me to teach him to play a flop shot as he had seen it being played on TV by top professional golfers. I was very sceptical about meeting his needs, as I believed it was way beyond his current ability and instead wanted to focus on helping him learn to play a simpler, more functional chip with a lower flight trajectory. However, I knew that the itch needed scratching and consequently, showed him how to play the shot. I then said he should go ahead and practice while I went to the bathroom. On my return, I found one very frustrated player, who had failed to get one ball up in the air. I then explained how the level of tariff of the shot was incredibly high and asked if he would like to learn to play an easier shot that would give him far more success. He smiled and said, "yes, please!" Sometimes, coaches need to allow the player to fail to work out the way forward, highlighting that the ability to align coach and player intentions is part of the art of designing CLA sessions.

Physical Constraints

When working with golfers, anthropometric factors such as body size and physical factors such as strength or flexibility are always important constraints to consider. For example, for young golfers, hole lengths need to be adapted to maximal hitting distances or alternately, par needs to be adjusted. In the beginner-level chapter, we will discuss this idea in more detail when we describe 'Tiger par'. Adult players may wish to take a similar perspective that we propose for the youngsters and view par on each hole as adjustable based on their own hitting ability.

Psychological Constraints

As any golfer knows, psychological factors such as emotions and confidence play a huge part in golf performance. The impact of nerves or fear of failure can be very significant for golfers of all levels and are often associated with specific places in golf rounds. For example, the golfer who has hit into the water on a long par 3, or a fear of specific demanding tee shots that do not 'fit' their swing can often tighten up due to negative thoughts. Similarly, every player knows that making a four-footer to win a tournament or to save par is different from hitting the same shot when the outcome has little impact, whilst, the high handicapper knows that chipping over a bunker onto a narrow green is much more difficult than if the same shot was from just off the front of the green with no hazard in the way (or in the mind). Why are psychological constraints so impactful on performance? Well, first, when our emotions are strongly engaged, our intentions change, we see the world differently and we move differently. To illustrate this point, consider the golfer who has historically struggled with a specific shot and is apprehensive even as (s)he is walking towards the ball, knowing the shot is imminent. When we are anxious or worrying about our ability to successfully complete a task there is a tendency to misperceive environmental information and fail to account for it in our decision-making. Further, we move differently and tend to 'freeze' up our movements: we can literally tighten up. Often there is a lack of flow in the golf shot taken in these emotional states and this often manifests itself as a jerky or shortened swing when faced with a challenging shot such as hitting over water. Similarly, the evidence suggests that when faced with comparable chips of the same length where the only difference is a bunker being present between the flag and the ball, high handicap golfers have a greater tendency to fluff the shot with the bunker in the way and often hit it straight in the sand. The tightness accompanying anxiety often leads to a failure to follow-through resulting in a 'stabbing' action. Coaches should be highly sensitive to the psychological responses of individual players in relation to particular shots or situations and should, therefore, look to devise learning environments that design-in emotion-laden tasks so the player can learn to understand and adapt to these feelings and to develop confidence by improving the ability to succeed in such circumstances. One strategy a coach could use in these situations is to take away the fear of failure by promoting exploration and promotion of motivational climates that encourage 'having a go' at it rather than 'avoiding' fearing a show of incompetence (Renshaw et al., 2012). Of course, sometimes simply exposing a player to a situation will not lead to improved performance and a coach may be advised to work with an accredited sport psychologist to provide the player with strategies to help adapt to these feelings and thoughts.

Environmental Constraints

Constraints in this category can be separated into Physical and Sociocultural Constraints. Physical environmental constraints include the surface from which the ball is hit, the wind, temperature, and altitude, as well as the access and availability of local courses and practice facilities. Sociocultural constraints include other people and therefore golf values, the ethos of the golf club, the individual coach and their expectations, family support, and, of course, the access to play on the courses available (see Ballesteros' story). On a more macro level, when looking at the potential playing population and the likelihood of young players taking up golf, the cultural capital of golf in countries, states, or regions (i.e., how much value is placed on being a golfer in those environments) can act as significant constraints on childrens decision to take up the sport (Araújo et al., 2010).

Wind

An example of an environmental constraint that perhaps places significant demands on the skill of the performer, more than any other, is wind. Scores rise in windy conditions, with research by Hunt (2018) showing that when the wind is practically nil (7 mph or less), the standard deviation of scores in a Tour event is roughly 2.2 strokes. In contrast, when the wind increases to 13 mph, the deviation increases to 2.5 strokes and when the wind reaches 20 mph, 3.3 strokes. It is my observation (GM) when working with amateur college-level players (Handicap range +2 to 9) that the most accomplished players are more able to modify their technique to minimise the effect that the wind has on their scoring and they are able to do so quickly. From a damage limitation perspective, the speed at which you are able to adapt your technique, when conditions change, is vitally important. In my experience, less-skilled players take far longer to find a solution, which is often too late and at a point where their score has already been fatally damaged. The more accomplished player has greater dexterity when it comes to finding a solution to the wind problem. For example, when playing into a headwind, I see our higher handicap College players try to hit the ball harder which makes the ball spin more, affecting their ability to control the distance the ball travels. Conversely, the more accomplished player tends to club down (use a longer club) and swing slower, thereby reducing the spin rate in the wind resulting in better distance control. However, slowing your swing down at will isn't easy as it is likely to be quite different in speed to your normal (preferred) tempo. Changing your tempo takes a lot of practice and highlights the importance of repetition without repetition to allow a player to find the most functional solution. Hence, experts find it easier to move into a new coordination pattern than non-experts when an environmental constraint such as wind is potentially perturbing them. Consequently, players and coaches need to look for opportunities to play in the wind whenever they can. The more a player is exposed to such conditions, the more accomplished he/she will become in dealing with them. Top players are aware of the importance of practising in conditions that they will face in competition. For example, Tiger Woods often visited Ireland as part of his preparations for the Open championship. According to Woods playing in Ireland was a key part of his preparation for the British Open as it allowed him to reacquaint himself to the demands of playing links golf. He reports: "It's been so much fun to play these type of golf courses and we play in all different types of weather which certainly makes it interesting…and I think it's instrumental in my preparation for the Open championship."

(https://www.irishgolfdesk.com/news-files/2014/7/1/tiger-for-pre-open-warm-up-in-ireland-it-might-not-be-a-bad-idea)

As we discuss later in the book for a player to exploit their true potential, they need to be able to spontaneously adapt their movement patterns as information (such as wind) nudges them into and out of different coordinative states. Crucially, the more accomplished the golfer is, the more able he/she is to do this on a moment to moment basis by quickly calibrating or 'tweaking' their 'techniques' to retain a level of stable performance.

Task Constraints

Task constraints are the easiest for coaches or teachers to manipulate as part of their practice (Tan et al., 2012). Task constraints include instructional constraints, rules of the sport, task demands such as the distance to the hole, the current status of the individual in the competition, any modified rules added on by the practitioner, modifications of equipment such as clubs or ball type. Manipulating constraints comes easily to many coaches, being a staple part of practice designs for many. For example, in our experience, many coaches who wish to develop a player's ability to hit 'long iron' approach shots choose to remove all woods from the player's golf bag. The likely result of this task constraint manipulation will be an increase in the distance required for the approach shot and promote the need to use a longer iron for the shot. Manipulating task constraints to provide players with opportunities to practice specific scenarios can enhance the value of practice and provides practitioners with a way to simulate the game demands representative of the competition environment. In the first book of this series we provided coaches with guidelines to support the implementation of a CLA and devoted a whole chapter to CLA golf coaching. In this book, we will provide many examples of how coaches can manipulate task constraints with players of all levels. However, throughout we will demonstrate the importance of considering how the different categories of constraints interact in a dynamic manner. We will discuss this point in the next section.

The Interaction of Constraints and Implications for Golf Coaching

As movement skills emerge from the interactions of key constraints in learning situations, golf coaches need to consider the dynamic interactions that are taking place during learning and performance. To provide an exemplar of how constraints interact to shape perception and action skills, consider the mid-handicapper (let's call him Sam) standing on the tee on a 150 m par 3 that requires a 140 m carry over a pond directly in front of the pin. There is an option to 'lay-up' to the left of the pond, which would leave a 20–30 m chip. There is also a bunker on the right and out of bounds 10 m behind the green. Normally, the wind is slightly behind on this tee and the distance is perfect for Sam's 6 iron (his favourite club). Sam generally plays to handicap on the hole and on a very good day, makes par or even has a birdie chance. Confident in his ability, he knows that a full smooth swing will end up with the ball sitting comfortably on the green, or at worst on the fringe with a relatively easy chip. However, on this particular day, the wind is gusting and blowing strongly into his face and although the hole is definitely playing longer, how much longer is difficult to work out. As soon as he walks up to the hole, Sam is struggling to decide on which club to take and his decision is impacted by the fact that his confidence in his 5 iron is low and he knows using his 4 hybrid increases the risk of him going over the back of the green and out of bounds and decreases his likelihood of hitting the green as his accuracy is poor with this club. He considers the option of laying up with his 6 iron but appreciates his chances of making a par are then greatly diminished as his chipping is OK, but not top notch. In the end, Sam decides to go with his 5 iron with the intention of hitting a 'bit harder' to make sure he clears the water. Whilst Sam has clarified his intentions and committed to the shot, he has failed to account for the increased anxiety level and the commensurately increased tension in his upper body. Consequently, his swing was shorter and lacked 'flow' and he ended up with a lesser distance than he would have achieved on a 'stress-free' 5 iron. Holding his breath as the ball travelled towards the hole, he thought he might have got away with it, but groaned as the ball hit the bank of the pond and rolled back into the water.

This example highlights how the individual, task, and environmental constraints interact on every shot (see Figure 1.9 for another example) and that coaches need to consider that each player they work with will have unique requirements. Consequently, in order to develop well-constructed CLA sessions, it is essential that coaches have a well-developed awareness of the range of the key constraints underpinning skilled performance so they can take into consideration constraints that are outside their control, as well as knowing which constraints they can deliberately manipulate with the aim of supporting the developing functional movement patterns and promote sound decision-making. To support this knowledge base, we suggest that golf coaches should develop a 'constraint builder' in line with the table we provided earlier (see the foundation book for a more extensive discussion of the key tools that can be used to support session design).

When choosing which constraints to manipulate, coaches need to determine the main factor limiting current performance. In the example above, perhaps the most important rate limiter is Sam's lack of practical intelligence in not recognizing that a 4 is a great score on this hole for a mid-handicapper playing into a strong headwind and that the 'field' will average a 4 on that hole in these conditions. His handicap category will probably average even higher (4+). Sam only needs to hit the green in 2 and then 2-putt to beat the field, if he single putts then, bingo! So perhaps his anxiety is coming from his perception of the challenge – which he is reading incorrectly. A key requirement in coaching is, therefore, recognizing the key rate limiters acting on the player. Below we move onto discussing rate limiters in more detail.

FIGURE 1.9 Constraints Interact. The task constraints of the second shot on the 5th Hole at Brisbane Golf Club has the potential to create strong emotions for the golfer who is drawn to the water. This is especially problematic for the right-hander who draws the ball or the lefty who fades it. Add in a strong right to left wind and emotions and thoughts intensify the psychological constraints and for some golfers leads to freezing of the degrees of freedom and a 'tight' swing.

Rate Limiters

A coach's choice of which constraints to initially manipulate is determined by his or her understanding of the key factor that is acting as a 'rate limiter' on the emergence of higher levels of performance of the golfer. Traditionally the term 'rate limiter' is associated with motor development and is typically used to describe how the relatively slower rate of development of a specific subsystem can act to prevent a new behaviour from emerging. For example, a lack of leg strength (captured in the muscle to fat ratio) can delay the onset of walking in babies (Thelen & Smith, 1996). However, these ideas can also be applied in golf coaching and in this context, rate limiters may include individual constraints such as size and maturation in junior golfers. Other potential rate limiters include environmental constraints such as limited opportunities to practice in specific conditions or an opportunity to receive high levels of coaching. Task constraints that can act as rate limiters could include not being able to practice on championship length courses and, hence, never learn to hit 'long' irons into the green. The key to effective coaching is about identifying the most significant 'rate limiter' on a player's performance so the coach can begin to create practice activities in which the learners must discover and experiment with different movement solutions (Chow et al., 2006). In summary, understanding how golf shots emerged and shaped under the influence of interacting constraints processes should inform the design of learning environments to enable learners to develop functional coordination solutions.

The Implications for Practice

So, what do the ideas of CLA suggest about the best ways to become a good golfer? To help coaches put the ideas of CLA into practice, we developed the Environment Design Principles (EDP), which we introduce and describe in detail in the foundation book of this series (Renshaw et al., 2019). The EDP consist of four principles that capture the core theoretical foundations of ecological dynamics (ED). The key principles are: (1) Session intention, (2) Constrain to Afford, (3) Representative Learning Design (RLD; including purpose and consequence), and (4) Repetition without Repetition (which is framed around manipulating variability to enhance adaptability and increase or decrease (in)stability). The key guiding principles for each concept are shown below in Figure 1.10 and Table 1.2.

While each principle is valuable in its own right, it is through the integration of all four principles that the framework is able to operate effectively and efficiently. In this book we will demonstrate how golf coaches can base CLA design on these principles in their practice, but for a more detailed dive into the overarching framework, the reader is encouraged to read the relevant sections in the foundation book.

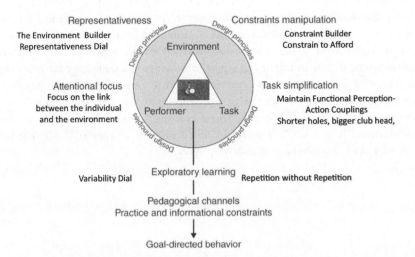

FIGURE 1.10 Coaching golf using a CLA involves the application of pedagogical principles of a nonlinear pedagogy (adapted from Button et al., 2020). We deal with each idea in the book.

TABLE 1.2 Environment design principles and guidance for implementation (Renshaw et al., 2019)

CLA principle	Description
1 Intentions	*The intentions of the session act as an overriding and organisational constraint.*
2 Constrain to afford	*'Design-in' constraints to offer/invite/encourage learners to explore the opportunities for action related to the session intention.*
3 Representative design	*Ensure that what the learners are seeing, hearing, and feeling in the practice environment is similar to the performance environment.*
4 Repetition without repetition	*'Design-in' the appropriate amount of variability and (in)stability to the practice environment.*

Chapter Summary

Successful golf performance requires an ability to adapt to the multiple, messy, chaotic situations that arise on the golf course (Evans & Tuttle, 2015). For example, in a four-day tournament, a golfer may play a specific hole completely differently each day due to the interaction of environmental conditions such as weather conditions (i.e., different wind directions and force, rain on some days, different green speeds, different cup locations). There may be effects of task constraints (i.e., where the player is sitting in the tournament and how this impacts his need to score on the hole), as well as changes within the individual golfer (i.e., level of nervousness, tiredness, fatigue, confidence, attentional focus, mild injuries, such as muscle strains and soreness). Playing good golf is, therefore, much more than just learning to swing the club in the same way over and over, but more about adapting that swing to the specific context that can change rapidly. As we highlighted earlier in the book, whilst we fully appreciate that learning to swing the club is an important aspect of developing a golfer, we advocate that this type of learning needs to occur in context to help the learner to develop a functional relationship with the performance environment. In this book, it is the preparation of a golfer for all of these eventualities that is our focus. We will demonstrate how a CLA is perfectly suited to such an approach whether it is working with beginners or elite-level players.

2

THE BEGINNER GOLFER

Introduction

Building on the introductory chapter where we described the key ideas of a CLA to golf, this chapter will focus on how to use a CLA to underpin coaching with beginners. We will discuss how a CLA can inform the coaching of children and adult beginners, regardless of age and ability. Adopting a CLA means that the key common principles remain the same. Ensuring that each lesson is matched to the current needs of the individual is an essential part of this process. Perhaps the key individual constraint that shapes learning design is not age but individual constraints, in terms of the potential time 'left' in a new player's career and the potential for growth. While we would not put any limits on a player's ambitions due to age, an older player has more barriers to their ultimate level of achievement. Of course, the goals an individual has and the time they can put into golf is unique to him/her which also shapes all the coaching interventions.

To set the scene, we will begin by describing how adopting a CLA with junior golfers can support the journey to elite status. Specifically, we will tell the story of how the fathers of Adam Scott and Tiger Woods underpinned their coaching by adopting many of the ideas inline with a CLA[1]. We will then provide a brief overview of the key concepts captured in their journeys and describe how they align with key concepts when implementing a CLA with beginners. We will then move on to discussing the learning process for beginners, focussing on the first lesson in the context of the degrees of freedom problem (Bernstein, 1967), information collection, the role of instructions, and briefly the importance of practising on the course. We finish with an exemplar Case Study of a mature beginner, Valerie, who recently came to see Pete when on the verge of giving up the game before she had even really started, before summarising the ideas raised in this chapter by providing some key thoughts and recommendations.

CLA in Junior Golf: Building the Foundations for Future Success

The journeys of great players are fascinating for many golf parents and coaches who are looking for potential insights they can use to inform their own practice. So, if we are interested in employing a CLA approach when coaching youngsters, is there anything we can learn from looking at what champions did when they were beginners? We believe that the answer is, yes, and we will start with the story of Adam Scott and his father, Phil, before moving on to tell the tale of the Tiger.

The Adam Scott Story

The story of how Phil Scott helped Adam become one of the best players in the world provides some great pointers for those working with beginners and developing players. We will frame our comments around an interview Phil gave just after Adam had won the 2013 US Masters that captures the essence of Scott's performance trajectory (Clark, 2014).

The Adam Scott Story

Introduction: Here is 2013 Masters Champion and former world No. 1 Adam's Scott's dad on the way Adam learnt to play golf. Adam's dad Phil was a PGA pro.

Interviewer: And then Adam came along. At what age did you first put a golf club in his hands?
A real club, probably five. Before that it was plastic clubs, whatever was around. Toy clubs (see Figure 2.1). About five and six, he and I started going to a par-3 course in Adelaide).

FIGURE 2.1   You can't start too early. Modifying equipment is a great way to create fun and success for even the youngest player.

Which course was that?

I called it North Adelaide Par 3. I'm not sure actually what it's called. It's an unbelievable facility there. There's two public courses and a par-3 course right next to Adelaide Oval and Memorial Drive. It's the most outstanding facility. So that's where we went at five years old. And he was good at it straight away.

What did you emphasise when you were teaching him how to play the game?

Adam and I played cricket and handball and tennis and racquetball. Anything that we could play. It was sport and golf was part of it. Playing golf, because I did and his mum [Pam] did, it was natural enough. But I encouraged it. Early on I had him hitting a large ball. And that's one of the things I really attest to. People try to push their kids along now. I made it easy. When he was a really little kid and he was swinging a plastic club, he used to hit a beach ball. My point being: how do you miss a beach ball? You can't! So it was always fun to him because he could hit it. And then we just brought the size of the ball down. So by the time it got to even playing par-3 golf, he was confident. He hit every shot great, but he was confident because he was used to hitting it.

So you taught him the proper grip, stance?

All the normal things. There was no complication to it. We had fun and that was the key. It's often overused, but I know Adam's said it over time in chats he's had with people that golf was always fun as a kid. And that's how we did it. It wasn't, 'Right, you've got to hit this perfect 80-yard shot on this par 3' and 'we're going to record every score.' We just had a ball, just like we did when we went out and kicked the footy at night. We just had fun.

Was there anything you emphasised early on, either technically or mentally?

I don't think we did a lot of mental things, outside of just understanding it was a game. And that's probably something I emphasised to him all his golfing life. It's just a game. You might want to be really good at it. It might be serious like now, it might be at the highest level or it might be big business, or it might be a lot of pressure with TV. But it's just a game. I did emphasise technical but in a simple way. Based on the line: if you're trying to hit a good shot, your chances increase if you do things correctly. So if you grip it right, stand right, get in to this type of position at the backswing and this type of position at the end of the swing, your chances of hitting a good shot have increased. So why wouldn't you do that?

You mentioned Adam's interests apart from golf. You had him playing a range of sports?

Yeah, he played everything. He did what every other kid was doing until he was about 13. He played Aussies Rules, tennis, cricket — and throwing stones. Anything where there was a game on, he was in.

So, is only one example still not convincing you of the merits of considering the developmental histories of top golfers? How about if we delve into the development of arguably the greatest player that has ever touched a golf club. Perhaps the story of one Mr Eldrick Wood's (or Tiger Woods to you and I) development might help convince you!

The Tale of the Tiger

Much like Adam Scott's dad, Tiger's dad, Earl, made the task simpler and fun for Tiger as a child. In conjunction with Tiger's first coach, Rudy Duran, Earl devised a scoring system that was fairer for Tiger. Tiger started playing mainly on a par 3 course where the real par was 54, however, Earl and Rudy devised 'Tiger Par', which was based on the distance Tiger could hit the ball. Consequently, at the start 'Tiger Par' was 67, with the par for each hole matched to Tiger's hitting ability. Of course, as Tiger grew and began to hit the ball further, Tiger par was adjusted downwards.

Another key idea behind Earl's philosophy of teaching Tiger from two years of age was that he taught him by starting on the green and then progressively worked back to the tee. Essentially, it would seem that Earl intuitively understood the ideas of *task simplification* and the *degrees of freedom problem* (see later). That is, he started with putting and finished with tee shots. The driver was the last club that Tiger learnt to hit. As Earl noted in his book 'Training a Tiger' (Woods & McDaniel, 1997) he strongly believed in Task Simplification:

> I firmly believe that in order to teach the full golf swing, you must start with the simplest golf swing, the putt, and then move on to chipping and pitching. That progression of instruction is the easiest way to teach a child how to play the game because it does not require major ball-striking ability. Golf should be taught from the green back to the tee...The swing is built from the green back to the tee. With proper training, practice, and dedication, 95 percent of the golf swing will be in place before your child ever takes a full swing.

The interview with Phil Scott and the story of how Earl Woods 'Trained a Tiger' reveal that there are several areas where their coaching methods were closely aligned to key principles of a CLA when working with beginner golfers, including the importance of framing learning around intentions, task simplification, and the interlinked degrees of freedom problem. Additionally, Phil Scott's comments raise some interesting points on the role of instructions in a CLA. We will discuss each of these concepts but first we will set them in the context of the learning process for beginners.

The Learning Process for Beginners

When a beginner is faced with the challenge of learning a new skill, the initial focus is on attempting to find a functional solution to solve the problem.

Essential to continued interest and motivation is the provision of learning tasks that facilitate success and lead to increased intrinsic motivation. Note how this focus aligns with Earl's ideas on starting with manageable coordination tasks for a young child, before moving on to more complex ways of organising motor system degrees of freedom. The task must, therefore, capture the imagination of the learner and meet their goals. A key tenet of implementing a CLA is Principle 1 from our EDP, the consideration of session Intentions, which "act as an overriding and organisational constraint" (Renshaw et al., 2019). For us, the two dads made the excellent decision to focus their early coaching on learning how *to play golf* and not on learning how *to swing a golf club*, which from our own experiences can turn off young players who get bored very quickly. Immediately setting challenges gave the boys purpose and provided consequences for their actions. Cleverly, learning activities were constantly adapted to match ability levels. In different ways, both used the principle of *Task Simplification* to achieve this goal. Task Simplification is defined as "systematically modifying the task constraints to provide a challenging task without sacrificing RLD (i.e., preserving important information–movement couplings)" Button et al., 2020, p. 238). For example, early on, Phil challenged Adam to hit a large beach ball with oversize plastic clubs, thereby maintaining the coupling between the information (the ball) and the movement (swinging the golf club). Similarly, Earl Woods used the idea of starting on the green rather than the tee, meaning that the task was much simpler as the club (the putter) was easier to control as it only needed to be moved a 'short' distance for achieving the task goal. In this case, information (the need to control distance and direction) and movement are coupled as the nature of the task gives meaning to the movement – in this scenario information implies what needs to be learnt. Cleverly, as Tiger improved, he moved him further and further away from the hole and required him to swing the club further and further. Progressively, Tiger's father was adding complexity to the situation rather than complication as moving further away from the green brings in course hazards and boundaries layering elements of strategy and decision-making to the learning environment. This approach maintained the crucial information–action relationship in practice designs. In this case, Tiger is also learning to play with all 'representative' information sources present and flowing. Earl Woods and Phil Scott seemed to have an intuitive understanding of how to solve the *degree of freedom problem* – that of harnessing the pattern forming tendencies of the human movement system that is capable of spontaneously adjusting to meet the demands of increasingly complex tasks.

The Degrees of Freedom Problem

Understanding how humans coordinate their actions when undertaking tasks such as keeping a stable posture while swinging a golf club to hit a ball towards a very small target is a key goal for motor learning scientists. Eminent Russian physiologist, Nikolai Bernstein (1967) was a key figure in attempts to answer such questions and was particularly interested in working out how the many micro-components of the human movement system such as muscles, joints, and limb segments work together to support the performance of complex tasks. This became known as the degrees of freedom problem. Degrees of freedom are defined as the "independent components of a system that can fit together in many different ways" (Button et al., 2020, p. 39). In golf, many different configurations are needed to 'successfully' play a round. For example, golfers need to (re)organise parts of the body to (1) create significant club head speed to hit booming drives off the tee, (2) shape a ball around a tree to hit the green, (3) have a fine touch to hit a delicate flop shot from the rough, or (4) control force to make a fast 2 m downhill putt.

How then are we able to control our actions given all the potential movement possibilities available to us? Bernstein's (1967) seminal insight was that movement is function-specific and not muscle-specific, a dominant idea in Russian physical education theory for some years. For Bernstein, it is the task that builds the action and not the other way around, that is, the implication is to learn a functional movement first, then attempt to apply it to a task. A simple example of this is if you give a child a tennis ball and ask him/her to throw the ball over an object such as a garden fence, he/she is capable (without the addition of explicit instructions or corrective verbal feedback) of spontaneously organising hundreds of bones and muscles and millions of muscle fibres to meet the demands of the task. If you then ask them to throw the ball in such a way that the ball bounces once on the ground before clearing the fence, he/she will spontaneously organise body parts into a different configuration to produce a different movement pattern to meet these new demands. This motor learning process has been called 'skill adaptation' (Araújo & Davids, 2011) (see Chapter 1). Crucially, what these two different movement patterns have in common is a clearly defined task goal (also See Figure 2.2 for an example of how the task builds the action). If the child does not know what the *intention* of the throw is, how would they know how to organise movement? Setting an outcome goal acts to *invite* the child to organise its movements in pursuit of the goal. This example emphasises the need for context in learning and intentions can 'frame' practice contexts first and foremost. It is the reason we spend so much time carefully constructing and defining the nature of the task we challenge our students to perform. This powerful learning tool is still considered to be a radical approach to helping people perform more effectively, despite the prominence of these ideas for the past 25 years in the motor learning literature. In summary, action (technique) is the emergent property of our individual interpretation of how to perform a task and is the reason why we see so many tour players with such radically different interpretations of how to move the club around their bodies.

The First Coaching Session

Building on previous discussions, I (PA) will now spend some time describing how I would frame an initial coaching session when working with beginners. Given that beginners are at the coordination stage (Renshaw et al., 2019) of

FIGURE 2.2 The task builds the action. Setting an outcome goal of landing the ball in the hoop acts to invite the beginner to organise their movements in pursuit of the goal. In the figure above, adding in a task constraint of three balls one-foot length in front or behind the ball means that the swing is adapted to be steeper or shallower to ensure that the three balls are not hit.

learning, coaching intentions are shaped around the two initial goals that most novice golfers tell me they want to be able to do; (1) hit the ball and (2) get it in the air. Once the player has done that, I begin to work towards learning to control force and direction (at a very simple level). In aiming to meet the player's goals I want to build confidence, as so many beginners think that it is going to be too hard for them. Using my knowledge of degrees of freedom and task simplification, I begin on the green using the putter. My intention is for the player to 'get to know' his/her tool (the putter) and I set tasks that get the player to explore how a club behaves and impacts the ball. To encourage exploration, I use CLA Principle 4: Repetition without Repetition (advocated by Bernstein (1967) to 'design in' the appropriate amount of variability and (in)stability to adapt to the context of the practice environment, to help the player to find the tool that best fits him/her.

To achieve this goal, I provide a range of putters with different lengths, different grip widths, and different head types. I encourage the player to swing each club to get a 'feel for it' and then go onto the practice green and simply hit lots of putts. To increase awareness of how different types of contact impact the roll of the ball, I use CLA Principle 2: Constrain to Afford, by adding markings to the ball (see Figure 2.3) to encourage the learner to explore how club contact with the ball impacts how the ball rolls. For example, the ball on the left (in Figure 2.3) is used to increase the golfer's awareness of the direction of roll and to assess if he/she can get the ball to roll along the same axis. Supported by guiding questions (i.e., informational constraints), using the ball on the right (in Figure 2.3) invites recognition of the type of spin created on the ball for different contact points. The next stage of awareness training encourages the golfer to become perceptually aware of where the club head is making contact with the ball. This is important as understanding that striking the ball on different parts of the putter face will result in the ball coming off the club at different speeds and makes distance control very difficult. To begin to develop awareness, I once again 'Constrain to Afford', by spraying foot powder on the putter face and asking the golfer to hit a series of putts to a target. After each shot, we evaluate if the putt was short, long, or just right and look at the contact point. Following a few sets of shots, some golfers do not even need to look at the club head to know where they struck the ball and begin to have an increased awareness of the strike point. At this point, their feedback systems are being tuned to help them self-regulate during learning. They can take in perceptual information from, (1) the sound of the contact, and (2), the distance the ball travelled. The next stage is to look at how stance and ball position impact on the way the ball rolls. To do this, I ask the golfer to experiment with different stance widths and ball placement in the stance (back, middle, front). These combinations result in the player hitting the ball on the downswing, at the bottom of the swing or on the upswing and via questioning we invite the player to tell me how these different combinations

FIGURE 2.3   Adding marking to balls can enhance awareness of the effect of striking the ball in different places with different angles.

affect the ball roll characteristics. Of course, this is just a selection of awareness activities for putting and as the player progresses, I would move onto building awareness of the environment such as grass types, grain, slopes, and the impact of the wind on a putt. (We return to the topic of awareness in Chapter 3). The final activity we undertake is to take the ball 15 yards off the green and onto the fairway and ask the player to hit the ball to the flag with his/her putter. The idea behind this task is to require the player to swing the club more, taking a longer backswing and a longer follow through…we are now ready for Goal 2.

Now, we have demonstrated to the player that he/she can hit the ball solidly and confidently, we move on to Goal 2 'getting the ball in the air'. Often beginners think they need to use a 'scooping' action to get the ball into the air and I attempt to overcome this 'rate limiter' by emphasising that the club and its loft (the concept of loft on clubs often needs explaining) will automatically do the job if a normal swing is undertaken. I start at the same place as in the final putting task and have the player putt half a dozen balls to the flag to get the feel of the swing again. I demonstrate how the same swing can get the ball in the air by swapping in a 56° wedge and showing how the club reacts as I swing it through the grass under the ball and 'plop' the ball onto the green. I then ask the player to listen to the sound of the contact with the ball (and grass) and describe what it sounds like. I will then ask him/her to copy me (initially without the ball) and try to make the same sound as he/she swings the club through the grass. I then invite the player to play a few shots and observe the outcome. The key difference in this task, compared to putting, is that we want the contact point to be at the bottom of the ball and sometimes the player will initially 'top' it. If this happens, I add in extra task constraints to guide the search for and discovery of the most functional contact point. First, I would place a broken tee in the ground under the back of the ball (so the ball is 'resting' on the tee) and tell the player that the tee is a 'nail' and it needs to be 'hammered' into the ball by swishing the club. Additionally, I may put a dot on the ball with a felt pen and orient it so it can just be seen at the contact point where the back of the ball touches the ground. This is another example of how I design-in task goals (constraints) to shape the movement solutions of the player. To help the player understand how the loft of the club impacts the height of the ball flight, I then vary the club adding in a 7 iron and a 9 iron. Here, I don't want to add too much variability and completely destabilise the player. To guide me, I use the Variability dial (see Figure 2.4) and ensure that the task has a variability level in the green zone. If we are having success, we will finish by having the player hit over a bunker to the flag. Here, I make sure there is plenty of room between the flag and the bunker to encourage a smooth swing.

Once a basic swing is in place, we will then use some of the ideas as discussed in the previous section to help the player create awareness of contact points, ball flight, and spin, and the relationship between swing lengths and how far the ball travels. As soon as possible, we will turn these practices into games. For example, if we have more than one client, we will place balls at six 'tees' (two cones) off the

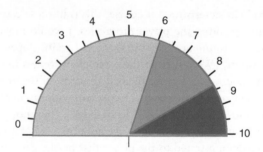

FIGURE 2.4 The Variability Dial. The dial can be used by the coach to make a conscious decision as to how much variability he/she wants to add into a task. The green zone (1–6) should be used when looking to build confidence and create stability in a movement pattern. The amber zone (6–8.5) should be used to create instability in the movement pattern to encourage exploration and the emergence of new movement solutions. The red zone (8.5–10) will create 'chaos' and should be used sparingly.

green and have them compete to get the lowest score for the 'round'. Here we are building up the game from 'the end' point (i.e., the key intention of getting the ball in the hole) and matching task demands to current ability.

Information Collection

Critics of a CLA have suggested that little importance is placed on what the coach says and has led to a CLA being wrongly characterised as a 'hands-off' approach to coaching. This is a misconception, as should be clear from our discussions so far. In CLA practice is considered as 'search'. Learners at all levels are being challenged to search for functional movement solutions during practice designs which use manipulations of constraints to guide the exploratory activities. The aim is not for the coach to undertake the search activities for the learner by 'telling' the golfer how to solve a movement problem. The golfer needs to be the one doing the searching! To support the learner's search, we do typically direct our verbal interactions differently than a more traditional approach. In traditional coaching, much of the focus is on verbal instructions and corrective feedback and is often directed at what the coach believes to be *the source* of the problem. For example, in the form of a swing change in pursuit of what is believed to be the 'optimal movement pattern'. As stated earlier, in a CLA, we do not adhere to the one-size-fits-all model or assume to know the 'correct' solution to the problem that the player is experiencing. Our initial interactions with players are, therefore, built around a search for information in a way that views each player as a dynamic system, with no two players ever being treated the same way. Understanding the work history, physical limitations, and sporting background of our players allows us to frame verbal interactions in a way that is unique to each learner and only to him/her. The background of the person in front of me shapes the language I use, often in the form of analogies or metaphors rather than through direct instruction. The aim is to create empathy and get our messages across in easily digestible ways. For example, when I (PA) coached Ian, who asked me where he should put the ball in his stance when hitting a 4 hybrid, I said to him "it depends" as that ball was part of a dynamic system that included the body and the environment. Consequently, the most functional ball position was dependent on how the different parts of the body were moving and also the lie of the ball. Due to his background in sport, he instantly got it. Of course, as mentioned earlier, instructions interact with task goals and we often manipulate task constraints to promote changes in technique. How we instruct is, therefore, a significant constraint closely tied to the task goals. We discuss their role now.

The Role of Instructions in a CLA

One point that we would like to make relates to the comments Phil Scott made in his interview, in that he emphasised technical skills "but in a simple way but can be playful and fun and made into a 'game'." Given the focus on promoting self-organisation and skill adaptation in a CLA, some commentators have suggested that instructions have no place in this process. However, we need to make clear that this is incorrect, and we are not against using verbal informational constraints when teaching some basic movement patterns. In fact, instructions are one of the most common strategies of coaches, whatever the approach, as they are presumed to facilitate the process of skill acquisition and aim to provide command and explanation for how a task such as hitting a ball to a target should be executed (Newell & Ranganathan, 2010). To clarify, from a CLA perspective, instructions act as a constraint that channel the learner's search for a functional solution to the task. However, it should be noted that instructional constraints can have a positive, neutral, or a negative impact on learning and performance. Instructions can act to exclude specific solutions so the coach must be careful not to delimit a golfer's search for his/her own functional solution. It is important to note that instructions that are too narrow and direct the learner towards a one-size-fits-all model of 'correctness' can actually be detrimental to learning (see the discussions later in the chapter for specific examples to explain this idea). Additionally, instructions cannot be considered without taking account of what the task is, as the interaction of instructions with the task will act to provide the boundaries that shape the attempted solution. Instructions can, therefore, be considered as information that should supplement the task constraints and high-lights the importance of ensuring that the task matches the current ability and needs of the learner (see Figure 2.5). Coaches need to work out if the learner is at the stage where he/she is attempting to develop 'coordination' or need to develop 'adaptability' (Renshaw et al., 2019). Consequently, practice intentions should be based on the stage of learning and provide the learner with a chance to search and explore to assemble a new coordination pattern problem, discover and stabilise new movement patterns, or 'exploit' a wide range of specific affordances in the

FIGURE 2.5 Instructions should be matched to the current ability level of the beginner and allow the learner to search and explore to assemble a functional coordination pattern. For example, in the short game area, the nearest three flagsticks should be used (alternately) and the player encouraged to use a range of clubs and experiment creating different ball flights.

environment enabling them to calibrate or tune actions to the specific constraints of the situation (Button et al., 2020).

Information provided by coaches can relate to the task goal or the movement pattern to be attained. In golf, there is often a focus on the movement pattern with the view that this will then determine the likelihood of achieving the task goal. With beginners, the instructions will mainly focus on promoting opportunities for exploration. In general, the ideas of a CLA would promote the view that task instructions should be based around the idea that coaches "should tell the player what to do not how to do it (Chow et al., 2015)." This means that the task should be framed around matching the outcome to the ability range of the player. For a youngster, instructional constraints may include visual demonstrations which should provide a ballpark image for the learner to explore and involve minimal or 'simple' instructions, a la Phil Scott.

RLD: Learning on the Course or at the Range?

Our final comment in this section is that it is our preference to coach on the course rather than the practice range, as we have seen dramatic changes in the client's thinking and behaviours when the focus of coaching switches to being about the outcome. When players ask themselves the question, "how do I get the ball in the hole in as few shots as possible" in contrast to "how should I swing the club" he/she looks to find the most functional solution rather than a more internal focus that often leads to negative thinking or 'freezing' of the degrees of freedom (of the joints and muscles involved). What, for many years, was commonly described as 'paralysis by analysis'. My ideas here, fit well with the CLA Principle 3: RLD. We will discuss the application of this principle in Chapters 4 and 5.

Having provided detailed coverage of how we frame our coaching with beginners when adopting a CLA, we will conclude with a real example of how Pete (PA) worked with Valerie, a senior beginner, to help her achieve her goal of being able to play a round with her husband, Jim.

Coaching Valerie using a CLA

Valerie came to me after being briefly coached by her husband, Jim. Valerie is in her early 60s and retiring following a 40-year career as a Maths teacher, she was taking up golf to keep active and spend more time with Jim during their retirement. Jim, a six-foot ex-rugby player has been a keen golfer all his life and plays off a 12 handicap. He has been very supportive of Valerie's interest in taking up golf, and when she expressed a keenness to take up golf he gave her his old full set of golf clubs. Using Valerie's story as an exemplar, first, I will outline the structure I (Pete) follow before working through a typical first session. I followed the procedures outlined above in my first session with Valerie. Chatting to her in the club house over a coffee, I found out that Valerie was five feet tall, had a slim athletic build and that whilst she played multiple sports growing up, she was mainly a hockey player. Valerie reported that she plays no other sport at the moment; however, she is physically active, takes their dog, Barney, for a long walk every day as well as attending a Yoga class every week. I ask Valerie about the coaching Jim has been giving her. She tells me that in the last few months Jim has had Valerie out on the golf course, but she confesses that she isn't enjoying it that much because she is struggling to hit the ball and it is taking her so many shots to get to the green. Valerie also reports that she is very conscious about the length of time it takes her to get around the golf course and can feel the frustration of other members and therefore she will only go out when the golf course is quiet. I asked Valerie what her goals would be from our sessions and she tells me she would just like to hit the ball a little better and further and if she could do that it would increase her enjoyment of playing golf. I take Valerie on the course to play a few holes and basically see all that she describes. She is struggling to hit the golf ball in the middle of the club face, sometimes misses the ball completely and consequently, her pace of play is not great. Valerie's frustration is clear and it is obvious she is not enjoying golf at all, and it was clear to me unless something changed, it most likely will lead to her giving up the game; I could tell from the way she spoke that it was something that was currently on her mind.

My first observation when watching Valerie play was that Jim's old set of clubs were completely unsuitable for her. As mentioned earlier, Jim is six feet tall and strong, and the clubs were fitted for his physique; consequently, they were too heavy and too long for Valerie. Therefore, the key initial rate limiter for Valerie was the weight and length of these golf clubs as they did not match her physical capabilities and were detrimental to her ability to move functionally. Fortunately, this was an easy fix and I knew we would see immediate improvements when I gave her clubs fitted to her slighter and smaller body frame.

For the rest of the session, I gave Valerie very light and shorter golf clubs and almost instantly she said; "this is so much easier to swing!" However, somewhat to my surprise, it did not improve her actual performance and her swing was still too inconsistent. Essentially, this was because the problem that Valerie had to solve was way too difficult for her size and current level of ability. Valerie was hitting off the tee box at the first hole on the Ladies tees at Craigmillar Park Golf Club, which is a par 5 of 401 yards long. Given that when she strikes the ball close to the middle of the club face Valerie can hit the ball 50 yards, this meant that the hole was seriously daunting and when I asked her, Valerie told me it normally takes her 10/12 shots to get to the green. Consequently, Valerie was over swinging the club as well as trying to hit the ball too hard and this was resulting in her swing being very uncontrolled and inconsistent. I used my knowledge of degrees of freedom and Valerie's background to explain the nature of the problem to her:

PETE: So in your Maths classes if you gave a pupil that is new to Algebra a really complex Algebra problem, how do you think they would fair?

VAL: Not very well at all.

PETE: And what if you gave them 18 of these really complex problems over the space of 3 or 4 hours. How do you think they would feel after this?

VAL: (smiling) Pretty much how I do after playing golf at the moment! Tired, de-motivated, frustrated and confused.

PETE: OK, so what would you do with this Maths student then Valerie?

VAL: I would make the Algebra problem easier, more in line with their abilities.

PETE: Voila! You see where I am going with this?

VAL: I surely do!

So, I played a really simple game with Valerie. I took Valerie to a position 20 yards out from the green and I asked her what she thought would be a reasonable score *for her* from here, given her current abilities. "5 shots," said Valerie. We play from there. After a few holes of playing this game, something really interesting happened. Without giving her any technical guidance or feedback on how to hit a golf ball, Valerie started hitting the golf ball more often in the middle of the face and the ball was getting into the air more often. She manages to score a 5, three times on the trot and then even scored a 4. So, what had changed? To answer that question, we need to go back and look at the reasons as to why Valerie was struggling in the first place. The key problem was that Valerie was inconsistent in striking the ball in the middle of the club face and getting the golf ball airborne; generally, the main objective for most golf shots out with the putting surface. Second, the task of hitting the ball from the tee was too hard for her current ability level, which resulted in her trying to hit the ball too hard, and consequently, over swinging the club. Third, the difficulty level was even higher due to the task constraints of requiring her to use golf clubs that were too heavy and too long. In summary, the requirement to try to hit beyond her capabilities and the use of inappropriate clubs was severely impacting Valerie's ability to construct a functional golf swing. In order to get the golf ball as far up the fairway as possible and play the hole in the least amount of shots possible, Valerie's solution was to over swing the golf club to try and generate the power to solve the problem in front of her. So basically, Valerie was over swinging a golf club that was too heavy for her body and it was not surprising that she had difficulty creating a functional golf shot. In essence, the key rate limiter (once the size and weight of the club were changed to match her physique) was the over swinging of the club which led to Valerie using more body parts (i.e., legs, hips, back) than she was capable of coordinating to try and hit the ball further. To that end, my first intervention, to have Valerie hit from 20 yards was focussed on the goal of reducing the length of her swing in order to enable her to develop a more consistent swing by reducing the degrees of freedom and the need to use so many body parts to hit the ball a long way (see Figure 2.6). By starting from 20 yards away from the hole, Valerie did indeed reduce the length of her swing and this allowed her to reach the green with one shot. By providing task constraints that were matched to Valerie's ability the task was made easier by removing the need for extra movements such as body sway that were an unwanted part of her over swings. In simple terms, the simplified task constraints of hitting over a shorter distance, using a lighter, shorter golf club allowed Valerie's golf swing to become much shorter, and made the club easier to control; consequently, she began striking the golf ball with greater consistency and success. In Valerie's words, the simplified task was akin to making the Math problem a lot simpler!

FIGURE 2.6 Designing practice where the task constraints are matched to current ability creates a simplified task where the golf swing becomes much shorter and makes the club easier to control. This improves consistency in ball striking and most importantly enhances motivation as the player has more success.

Afterthoughts: Changing Techniques without Explicit Instructions

My work with Valerie was based on the idea of task simplification rather than providing lots of technically oriented instructions. The key question then is – why do I adopt such an approach when the traditional view would be to tell the beginner what they need to do? In this section, I am going to describe what I have observed in terms of the impact of coaching by shaping the task rather than giving lots of technical instructions. First, in terms of the biggest impact, here is the key point; Valerie is now more intrinsically motivated because she is more engaged in the game of golf as she feels as though she is getting better. Valerie actually enjoys it; she feels that she can go out at any time with her husband now and not worry about being too slow. The game, and golf **is** just a game with problems to be solved, is now appropriately matched to Valerie's current level of ability. Another key point of this approach is that Valerie is learning to play on the golf course, and every shot she plays in practice has a purpose and consequence in line with playing golf rather than just hitting a ball with no performance consequence. By using such an approach, Valerie was able to see the progress she was making and became much more motivated. Essentially, because the tasks are more matched to her current level of ability, she is much more relaxed on the course and doesn't worry over what other golfers are thinking about her.

Final Thoughts: A CLA Is Back to Basics or a Conversation?

Some of the common questions I get asked when coaching golfers new to the game is when do you start actually 'coaching'? When are we going to start working on the basics? Basics, I presume refers to the grip, aim, stance, posture, ball position, backswing, downswing, and follow through. I have two stock answers when I am asked such questions, one, "I already have", followed up with, two, "anyway tell me what the basics look like given that a whole raft of grips are used by the top 100 players in the world." I contend that there is no one-size-fits-all solution for everyone, and therefore, adopting a CLA means that the coaching requires me to design practice tasks that lead to the emergence of functional solutions for that individual. If I can do this without giving prescriptive verbal instructions and feedback then so much the better, as working it out for themselves empowers beginners. Additionally, I have found that words can be misinterpreted, often due to a lack of understanding of the idea I am trying to get across or because I haven't explained it well enough. I have found that learning is much more natural if I can design tasks that lead to the emergence of functional coordination solutions that help the golfer achieve their goals. Framing this decision means I ask myself questions such as, (1) Is Valerie able to answer the question? (2) Do I need to ask a question to guide or direct exploration? (3) Does the conversation look as though it is getting Valerie's attention? (4) Is the conversation stalling because the question I have asked is too hard or too boring? (5) How should I reframe the questions given the answers Valerie is providing?

Often, I have to resist the temptation to stop the session to offer sage advice or provide specific instructions. Essentially, I found that doing this interfered with the learning process and made me realise I needed to give more time and space for the beginner to engage in the task to search and find their solution. I found this was a significant issue when I first started using a CLA as I knew the answer and my training as an instructor meant I felt almost compelled to give her the answer. However, over time I have found that allowing time for the player to search for solutions by supporting their exploration is a more effective way to promote learning of the basics (in fact all skills) as they emerge from the ongoing conversation. My goal in these sessions is to create curiosity and encourage a client to continue to explore away from the coaching session. I construct this ongoing exploration in terms such as asking clients to consider what they did when they wanted to learn something new as a child. Of course, I should qualify my answer here by saying that if there is a completely dysfunctional grip then I do use demonstrations and analogies to narrow the exploration process. By directing search and providing a limited range of options, I find that a lot of wasted time is avoided where clients come up with solutions that are actually dysfunctional. However, I will only resort to this approach if constrained by time (constraints of commercial coaching), and if it is going to add to the conversation and help them solve the task/problem. In summary, over the next few months/years for Valerie's game/task, I will keep having these conversations and developing the task to a developmentally appropriate level for Valerie.

Summary

Adopting Task Simplifications is something we would recommend irrespective of the age of the golfer and we discuss how to do this using the specific case study of Valerie at the end of the chapter. Key constraints to consider include the size and weight of the club and the length and difficulty of the holes being played. Individualising par a la Tiger par has much to be said for it and is a concept that players of any age or ability would benefit from using in their own game[2]. On a psychological level, developing a mindset where achievement is framed to current ability rather than on a 'norm' based on adult performance is very powerful and we believe can only help in providing a positive view of competence. In comparison, measurement of performance using a deficit model, that is, where you tell a player they are 'x' number of shots worse than the score expected of 'good players' (i.e., golfers who play to par or better) does not help promote self-confidence in emerging players. Our advice for the coach of any player would, therefore, be to work out how far they can hit the ball off the tee with their irons and develop specific 'par' for that golfer.

Key Messages and Recommendations

This chapter highlights some key messages for coaches and beginner-level golfers irrespective of age. These can be summarised as follows:

- The characteristics of an individual are unique and the way the player hits a ball is significantly impacted by this; movement has a history and the previous life, work, or sporting experiences of a golfer may be the main rate limiter to enhancing his performance.
  - The coach needs to find out as much about the player as possible to support the way he or she understands what he/she is seeing, what he/she asks the golfer to do and how he/she talks to the player.
- The difficulty of the task needs to be matched to the current skill level of the player.
  - Task simplification is a good starting point and is based on an in-depth understanding of the player's current abilities.
- There is no one correct or optimal solution to hitting a golf ball.
  - Coaches need to understand that the interaction between the individual, the environment, and the task is dynamic with the most functional solution constantly emerging. There are likely to be small but meaningful variations in the movement solutions initiated by all learners and so it is important for coaches not to have an 'ideal movement template' in mind (to which all learners need to fit).
- Task Constraints can be manipulated to shape the movement solutions
  - Wherever possible the coach should attempt to design the learning environment that supports the emergence of a functional solution without having to resort to instructions.
- Learning can be fun and exploratory
  - It's OK to have fun during learning and almost essential as a child player.
  - Coaches can create a climate where exploration and fun go together. In such an environment, a poor shot should not be seen as destructive, but an opportunity to learn or a challenge to overcome.
- Skills need to have context.
  - Make sure that learners have an 'intention' which frames their practice attempts (e.g., to lift the ball out of long grass or sand or to move the ball from A to B).
  - Coach golf, not golf swings by setting questions (games-based problems) that the golfer needs to answer with actions, not verbal responses.
  - Wherever possible this means setting the problem in terms of scoring on a golf course.
- Coaches' words are an important informational constraint.
  - Instructional constraints can definitely be used to promote a learner's search for a task solution

- Frame verbal interactions with the player to avoid golf jargon and communicate in a language that he or she understands. Analogies or metaphors can create empathy and get messages across in easily digestible ways.
- Give the golfer the time and space to learn
  - Resist the temptation to give the answer 'too soon'.

Notes

1 We need to make clear that we are not claiming that the two dads based their approaches on an explicit adoption of the CLA methodology. Simply that their approach mirrored many of the key concepts. Indeed, when we read Errol Woods' book, *Training a Tiger*, we were struck by how well Errol 'got' skill learning with many of his ideas fitting beautifully with the key ideas of a CLA.
2 We discuss this idea with respect to emerging elite players in the "So you want to play on the tour chapter?"

3

THE HIGH HANDICAPPER

Introduction

In this chapter, we aim to reframe the thinking behind the ubiquitous search of players and coaches for consistency by constantly *attempting* to repeat identical golf swing movements to the same target over and again in practice. Golfers, therefore, often treat coaching like a trip to the doctor to help cure their problems, with the prescription being repetitive technique rehearsal 'until the errors magically disappear'. However, playing good golf is about solving problems on the golf course and adapting to specific conditions and this requires a different frame of mind towards practice. Whilst, intuitively, the repetition *after* repetition approach seems appealing and is reinforced by statements such as 'perfect practice, makes perfect performance', we will demonstrate that to improve consistency high handicappers need to embrace several key concepts. First, variability in performance and scoring is normal, whatever be the level of the performer. Second, Nikolai Bernstein's work a long time ago with the task of swinging a hammer, ironically, showed that it is impossible to ever repeat the same movement and the time spent trying to achieve this is wasted time. Third, top golfers are more consistent as they can, (1) compensate for the variability in their swings, and (2) adapt to the many variable constraints encountered on the golf course. We will then describe how coaches can use a range of strategies to help high handicappers develop more awareness of their golf swing and develop their functional variability to be more consistent in their ball striking. We will also discuss how greater adaptability can be developed by applying the principles of a CLA in practice for golfers to *improve* their consistency. We finish with two case studies demonstrating how PA works with high handicappers in his coaching.

Beyond Curing the Golf Swing

Golfers often compare the role of the coach to that of a doctor with a focus on curing golf-related illnesses such as the slice, duck hook, or shank. Traditionally, upon visiting the 'surgery', the doctor (coach) will gather the symptoms by observation before prescribing the cure. Often, this cure is in the form of a prescription delivered by instructions and error corrections. As discussed previously, central to much of professional golf coaching is the aim of acquiring the perfect, repeatable swing. However, this model has some limitations if it fails to consider that the optimal moment solution should be in line with the individual's needs on a shot by shot basis. Coaching the high handicapper, therefore, needs to revolve around solving specific problems on the course, such as getting out of bunkers, developing a range of options around the green, or simply becoming more attuned to key affordances of the environment (i.e., hitting into the wind). As we have mentioned in the previous chapters, the key to providing an optimal coaching experience for a player is to consider the individual and the environment that he/she plays in as one 'system'. For the high handicapper, this performer-environment scale of analysis most likely revolves around learning to play on one course most of the time. For example, a high handicap golfer who is playing on tight links courses in Scotland will need to develop different abilities than one playing in America on wide, long courses (Figure 3.1). To restate, coaches must be aware that the environments in which a golfer learns and plays shape the specific abilities he/she will need to develop to be effective. In effect, using the example above, physical environmental features such as tight fairways will '*invite*' players to develop skills such as accuracy, possibly at the expense of power. Similarly, playing links courses invites players to keep the ball low and hit bump and run type approach shots, whereas a long golf course, which lacks wind and has many forced carries (i.e. water) will invite different solutions.

FIGURE 3.1 The Environment that a golfer learns to play in shapes the abilities he/she develops. A. The Scottish player tends to develop accuracy of the tee at the expense of distance due to the narrow fairways and high winds prevalent on links courses, whilst (B) the America player learns to fly the ball high into greens on park courses. (B is courtesy of Remco Polman).

The Myth of Consistency

As we highlighted in the introduction, we believe that many high handicappers are being held back by a mindset centred on trying to achieve consistency in inappropriate ways. In this section, we want to provide a better understanding of this topic in order to encourage coaches and players to move them beyond a 'repetition *after* repetition' approach common to much of current golf practice.

The word consistency is one I (PA) hear every day on the lesson tee, especially from high handicappers. 'I would just like to be more consistent', 'I want my swing to be more consistent.' Well, all I'll say is good luck with that! The key point made here is that consistency is a myth even for the very best golfers. To illustrate the point, let's consider the two parts of the goal of consistency, scoring and the golf 'swing'. Starting with scoring, let's compare the scores of Dwayne, a high handicapper, Ian, who is now a mid-handicapper, and some of the best golfers in the world in terms of their scoring and level of consistency off the tee and in hitting fairways and greens.

Dwayne started playing less than a year ago and plays once per week. As can be seen in Figure 3.2 whilst his handicap has decreased slightly, his scores for his last 20 rounds have a range of 15 shots (18–33).

One might not be surprised by the big differences from round to round, but what might we see if we look at a player who is clearly improving? Surely as his/her handicap comes down, he/she would be getting much more consistent in his scores. Let's look at this systematically, by first considering Ian's handicap and the variability in his scores, before looking at both sets of data together. Figure 3.3 shows (1) the strokes per round; (2) the handicap progression, and (3) shows the combined data. When considering strokes alone, the high level of inconsistency (17 shots) was in line with that seen in Dwayne's data and would suggest that Ian was making little progress (with one or two positive outliers). However, considering handicap alone (2) suggests that the player was making great strides and a fall of eight shots would be reflective of a player making great strides. Putting the data together (3) highlights that improved performance and consistency do not go together for an improving high handicapper.

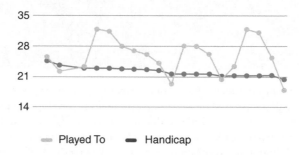

FIGURE 3.2 The range of scores and handicap for Dwayne.

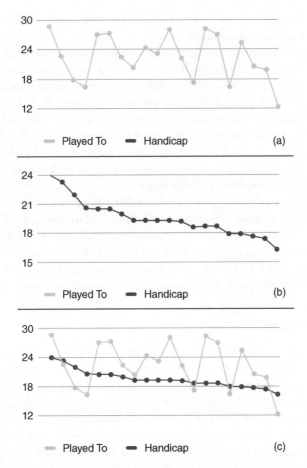

FIGURE 3.3 Ian's (a) Scores per round; (b) Handicap and (c) combined data.

So, what do the data tell us about consistency? The key point is that even when improving, players are still inconsistent. However, you may say, a 16-handicapper is still going to be highly inconsistent and elite level players would have much more consistency in their scores, wouldn't they? Well, no, they don't, and research has found that PGA Tour, LPGA & SPGA players' round-to-round inconsistency in performance is more the rule than the exception for players on the American professional tours (Clark, 2005). For example, in 2018, Justin Rose had an 11-shot difference between his lowest and highest scores (63–74), whilst Brooks Koepka had a 15-shot differential (63–78). In 2017, Justin Thomas had a 21-shot difference, with a low of 59(!) and a high of 80. Clearly, these scores are much lower than those of the high handicapper. We also need to consider that tour players are playing on longer courses, with more challenging demands and in different weather conditions. But the point is, they still demonstrate a similar range in terms of their scoring as their amateur counterparts. In fact, we would argue that Tour players are just as likely as the high handicapper to complain about wanting to be more consistent.

Now let's look at the issue of consistency from the other side of the same coin, variability, and debunk some myths about how 'perfect' professional golfers are when they hit the ball. What is the norm for tour pros and high handicappers in terms of their ball striking ability? According to Mark Broadie (2014), off the tee, the average male tour player misses his target by 3.4° while the 18-handicapper misses his by 6.5°. In reality, because (male) tour pros hit the ball further, this means a miss of 21 yards for a 300-yard drive, whilst the 90-handicapper, with an average drive of 225 yards misses his target by 25 yards. Accuracy is, therefore, not necessarily the key difference but distance is, as it leaves the pros with shorter shots into the green. It is also worth noting that Tour golfers also miss greens; on average 20% from 100 to 150 yards and 33% from 150 to 200 yards. What is clear, is that even experts have levels of variability that they are not happy with, but, what all golfers, and in particular high handicappers need to realise, is that variability is a fact of life. In fact, in terms of movement, variability can be an advantage. We discuss this more contemporary view of variability in the next section.

Movement Variability

An interesting question for coaches is why do scratch or tour players make better contact with the ball than high handicappers? Perhaps, surprisingly, the answer is that they have the capacity to be more variable in their swings. However, it's important to note that not all variability is good and we need to add the caveat, that tour players have more 'good' and less 'bad' variability. Let us explain.

Traditionally, in the motor learning literature, movement variability has been classified as 'error', with movement errors 'causing' high levels of variability in outcome performance. At a superficial level this idea would seem to make sense and perhaps underpins the traditional 'error detection' model of coaching. However, motor learning theorists argued that actually not all variability in performance is necessarily detrimental. With the advent of high-speed cameras, biomechanists are revealing that expert performers across sports actually demonstrate more variability in their movements. How can we square this apparently round hole? Well, let's move away from golf for a moment and look at a similar task, that of hammering a nail into a piece of wood using a hammer, similar to the analysis of the movements of blacksmiths conducted by Bernstein in the 1930s. Just like hitting a golf ball, hammering a nail requires swinging a tool to hit a stationary target. However, it could be argued that using a hammer is much easier, as fewer body parts (degrees of freedom) need to be regulated to achieve the task. So, what would we expect to see in terms of the consistency and variability in each consecutive hammer swing? I (IR) recently asked my students to complete this task by using their dominant and non-dominant hand. I wanted them to consider what they might see; so, before we completed the task, we made some predictions with regards to the difference in success rates and then tried to think of an explanation why this might be the case. As expected, students predicted a higher success rate with the dominant hand and explained this by the fact that the swings would be more consistent with this hand due to better control of the hammer, as they were used to doing things with their dominant hand. The results for one student are shown below (see Figure 3.4) and reflect findings from all students in the group.

In relation to our predictions, premise one was found to be correct with a success rate of 100% with the dominant hand condition and 70% with the non-dominant hand. However, the proposed reason for the better performance was found to be incorrect. If consistency in movement was the key, we would expect to see a very low level of variability in the start point of the hammer swings in the dominant condition. However, no differences were found between the two groups with a relatively inconsistent starting point being seen. However, the variability *in the end point of the swing* was much lower in the dominant hand, in comparison to the non-dominant hand condition, as reflected in the success rate. The interesting question for us then is how the student manages to achieve the task 100% of the time with the right hand, but only 70% with the left? The 'zeroing-in' of the hammerhead on the nail when using the dominant right hand, appears to show that the student was aware of where the hammerhead space was in relation to the nail and was, therefore, able to manoeuvre the head of the

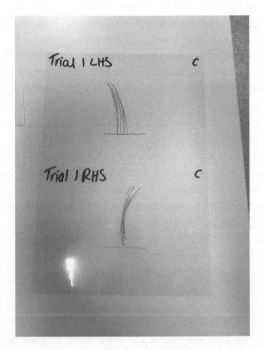

FIGURE 3.4 The path of the head of a hammer when hitting a nail into wood. Trial 1 LHS is the non-dominant hand and Trial 2 RHS is the dominant hand.

hammer by adjusting the wrist as he swung the hammer. However, when using the non-dominant left hand, this 'manoeuvrability' was not observed; that is, he could not 'correct' the position of the hammer during the swing. Notably, the student attempted to solve the problem by reducing the length of the swing and achieved some success with this strategy.

So, returning to golf, what can we learn from this study and how can we relate the findings to our understanding of the golf swings of high handicappers compared to experts? In particular, what does it mean for the traditional view of variability and the search for consistency in golf swings? The first key point is that, despite the task being much simpler than the golf swing, it was impossible to repeat an identical swing. This was even the case when the swings were consecutive without a break between each one. Think about this in terms of golf swings which might have many minutes between them. Additionally, golfers rarely use the same tool (club) twice in succession (except for going out of bounds of course!). So, what does this tell you about trying to replicate the same swing every time? Hopefully, you will realise that it is a pointless exercise and we can spend our practice time undertaking much more fruitful tasks.

The second finding that is interesting for golf coaches, was that successful hits with the dominant hand showed high levels of variability in the start point of the hammer, but low levels of variability in terms of the contact point with the nail. Successful contact, it would appear, is underpinned by the ability of the 'hammerer' to compensate for the initial variations in the start position of the hammer to bring the head into contact with the nail. Similar findings have been found across many sports and what has been termed *functional variability* appears to be a prerequisite to successfully intercepting any target. Here, this is what we meant by the term 'good' variability. In contrast, when trying to hit the nail with the non-dominant hand, there was less success with a much wider spread in the contact point (or not) with the nail. Here, it would appear that the hammerer did not have the capacity to adjust the head of the hammer during the swing. This type of variability is, therefore, dysfunctional. We call this 'bad' variability. One interesting observation was that because the hammerer could not get control of the hammerhead, they reduced the swing length. Effectively, they reduced the degrees of freedom to make the task easier by decreasing the total amount of variability. Compare this finding to the recommendations put forward in the previous chapter.

In summary, what these findings suggest for golf coaches is that high handicap golfers need to develop the ability to tap into more 'good' variability and decrease the amount of 'bad' variability in their actions. In the short-term, this can be achieved by shortening the backswing to decrease the total overall amount of variability (i.e. reduce the bad and decrease the amount of good variability needed) and make the task easier. This is exactly what PA did with Valerie and as recommended by Earl Woods. In the long-term, coaches need to work with high handicappers to develop the 'good' variability. This requires an awareness of where the club head is during the swing. We focus on this idea later in the chapter.

Dexterity and Degeneracy: A Platform for Skill Adaptation in Golf

An interesting caveat to my hammer time session (pun attempted ☺) was the conversation I had with one of the students during the lesson who informed me he was an ex-chippie. I encouraged him to tell his story to the other students and he spent ten minutes describing all the nuances of working with a hammer. Most interestingly, he talked about how the 'job' (i.e., intentions) shaped the way the hammer should be used and that this required him to have significant dexterity in the way he gripped it and swung it. He was hefting the hammer as he talked and described how its properties did not suit him as it was heavier and the centre of gravity was in a different place than in his own hammer. This attunement to the properties of a tool or piece of equipment has also been found in tennis players who use 'touch' or 'feel' (known as haptic information) when hefting or wielding a racquet to distinguish between one they preferred or did not like as much (Carello, Thuot & Turvey, 2000). As I listened to the student, I recalled a conversation I recently had with a very good golfer, who described how he manipulated his grip, the club face angle, the steepness and length of the swing to solve problems on the course. The ability to exploit the affordances of their tool (i.e., club), highlights the importance of 'dexterity' in skilled performance (Bernstein, 1967, p. 228). As we discussed previously in Chapter 2, the multiple degrees of freedom in the human movement system provide performers with the capacity to reorganise coordination to deal with changes in constraints. In a CLA, this idea is captured by the concept of degeneracy (i.e., "the ability of elements that are structurally different to perform the same function or yield the same output." (Edelman & Gally, 2001, p. 137). Degeneracy has been observed in the movement system and supports the interchange of different sub-structures (i.e., contributions of different body parts) in achieving a task goal. In an individual athlete, degeneracy involves the (re)organisation of different muscle groups, joint combinations, and limb segments (motor system degrees of freedom) to coordinate actions to achieve the same task goals. System degeneracy, therefore, underpins dexterity and provides great flexibility, adaptability, and robustness needed for an athlete's functionality during his performance (Davids et al., 2008). Hence, a golfer who shows greater dexterity is able to adapt to the changes in constraints such as different surfaces, slopes, fatigue or wind direction, or the current status of the competition.

The implication for coaches is that they should design practice tasks to ensure that golfers have plenty of opportunities for continually adapting their actions (reorganising their motor system degrees of freedom) to achieve same/different task goals under varying performance conditions (see Figure 3.5). Essential to this process is incorporating variability into learning contexts to encourage players to seek different solutions to the same performance problem, as well as requiring players to explore a variety of related task problems to find the same performance solution (Davids et al., 2008). Practice tasks should, therefore, consist of 'Repetition without Repetition' Principle 4 in our CLA design framework.

FIGURE 3.5   Developing adaptability by increasing a golfer's range of options. On the left, the drive requires a draw, a 'straight' shot and a fade. On the right, the chip requires different heights of ball flight. The golfer can be encouraged to use one club to create different ball flights or use a range of clubs. The goal is to develop a range of options to fit different conditions.

For example, repetition *after* repetition of the same movement pattern, such as attempting to hit the perfect 6 iron from the same spot, should be replaced with repetition *without* repetition. In terms of practice strategy, this principle can be used in many different ways. For example, golfers could be presented with different performance conditions that require them to hit the 6 iron from different places across the fairway, or out of the rough to fly the ball in low or high, or with a draw or fade. In essence, this change of focus means that learners should be challenged to repeat the process of solving the same performance problems under varied practice task constraints.

Variability (Can) Create Consistency

So, pulling this all together, what have we learnt about how to be more consistent on the golf course? It should be clear from the previous discussion that given that golf is played in a dynamic environment, reproducing the same swing every time would not actually fit these demands. At best the 'consistent' swing developed by repetition *after* repetition we see undertaken by many golfers at the range, might suit one specific situation, but actually, the key to consistent scoring is not about creating a robotically consistent golf swing, but one that shows degeneracy and can interact and adapt to the constantly changing conditions on the golf course. In fact, as we saw in the previous discussion, a key trait that is seen consistently in the best golfers is that they are highly adaptable in their movements in response to the varying conditions they face. Therefore, an expert golfer's consistency is not in the golf swing but in a more predictable or 'consistent' outcome from functional (i.e. they work) adaptations in the golf swing.

This game is always evolving, our court, our field of play, it always changes and it changes every day, one day it may be dry, one day it may be soft, because it rained or it might have a little dew on the ground, windy. All these different variables happen and you have to ADJUST and you have to be so ADAPTABLE at any moment, because it can change and your game plan changes too and you've got to be flexible in your game plan, and your mental strategy evolves as the day goes along.

(*Tiger Woods, 2017*)

So, can we redefine the word 'consistency' for golf? Maybe a better working definition would be:

Consistently adapting your golf swing to interact with the constantly changing field of play and consequently producing more predictable shot outcomes.

If we now use this as our definition, the look, smell, and feel of the training environment changes dramatically. However, I hear you say, that's all very well, but this is a high handicapper chapter! How do I become more 'consistent' if I can't even hit the ball off of a flat lie with some sort of predictability in my shot outcome? (see Figure 3.6). You can start by focussing on emphasising to the golfer that it is their game and they have to take ownership of it. We can do this by building awareness, something that the great players of the past were very focused on in their own careers.

FIGURE 3.6 On the course lies are rarely flat, so high handicappers need to create opportunities to play off different slopes to develop an understanding of what happens to ball flight when the ball is above or below your feet, or if you are hitting uphill or downhill.

Exploration: Building Awareness and Exploiting Affordances

An important skill for coaches is knowing how to help create learning environments that promote awareness. For the golfer, we wish to focus on building awareness of key affordances, such as the properties of the golf club, the grain or the undulations and slopes of greens, the wind direction and force, the quality of a lie, or any of the other myriad affordances found on golf courses. Designing learning environments to support enhanced awareness requires an understanding of the way individuals control movements and the subsequent impact of directing attention to make players more aware of their own body movements. Bernstein (1967) proposed four levels of control by the Central Nervous System; the lowest level is the level of Tone (for controlling posture and 'background' muscular forces'), followed by the level of Synergy (responsible for the coordinated movement that involves linking muscle groups), the level of Space (i.e. control of movement in space adjacent to the body that requires a perception of the workspace), and finally the highest level, Action (which include movements requiring action sequences and adaptive changes). Figure 3.7 brings together these ideas and provides a schematic showing how they can be applied to golf coaching. It is important to note that whereas all other levels function at a subconscious level, the highest level of control occurs at a conscious level and, therefore, only this level which involves the planning for the shot benefits from the use of explicit instruction or verbal feedback. Of interest for this book is that the set-up, control of the golf swing for the practice swing, and actually hitting the ball is at the subconscious level and coaching strategies need to align and allow learners to harness the self-organising movement system dynamics that are most functional for the task (Davids et al., 2008, p. 179). Coaches should, therefore, ensure that learners are not disrupted from their natural learning processes by verbal instruction or by an overfocus on specific body parts (Davids et al., 2008). This

Type of Control	Level of Control	Activity	Golf Activity	Coaching Strategy
Conscious	Action	Movements requiring action sequences and adaptive changes	Thinking, problem solving, coordinating actions with respect to specific golf contexts	The design of games, targeting cognitive activity (expressed through a tightly coupled perception-action relationship)
	Space	Control of movement in space adjacent to the body that requires perception of the workspace such as an interceptive action	Hitting a Golf Ball	Repetition without Repetition Allow movements to self-organise in a subconscious way
	Synergy	Co-ordinated movement that involves linking muscle groups	The Practice Shot: Swinging a golf club	Implicit Learning Awareness activities
Sub-Conscious	Tone	Postural Control and priming the system	Stance and Balance	'General enrichment of balance, postural control, regulation of upright stance'

FIGURE 3.7 Bernstein's Level of Control and guidelines for golf coaching.

is a significant point and brings into question the predominant use of explicit instruction methods that are currently the staple method for many golf coaches. So, what are the alternatives for golf coaches? In the next section we will attempt to provide some answers in the context of the need to promote subconscious (or implicit) learning when directing attentional focus.

Attentional Focus in Golf

One of the most important premises of a CLA is the fundamental role of information in guiding movement behaviours, especially during the process of learning; the direction of the coaches' attentional focus for golfers is therefore of significant importance. Coaches can direct search 'internally' to focus on bodily movements or 'externally' to the consequences of actions. Attentional focus has become a major topic in golf coaching and the debate rages between motor learning researchers who strongly support the idea of an external focus (Wulf, 2013) and coaches who are convinced that an internal focus is the most effective strategy (Montero et al., 2019). However, recent work has highlighted the difficulties in interpreting findings due to the numerous confounds in experimental tests (Montero et al., 2019) as exemplified with issues such as what counts as an internal or external focus often being blurred or whether the task instruction actually elicited the direction of focus intended. For example, focus on the golf club has generally been viewed as an external focus. However, Gibson (1986) suggests that once an implement is grasped, it becomes a tool and should thereafter be treated as part of the individual – an extension of a limb in contact with the tool. Indeed, many high-ability golfers report that the club becomes integrated into their sense of self and how they see and interact with the environment. Scientists have described this in terms of the tool as 'intimately integrated' into the body, and for the golfer, this means perceiving the world *through* the club (Rochat et al., 2019).

Given the tension between the two schools of thought, here we propose a new approach, one which focusses on enhancing the coupling between perception and action, or put another way, on interactions between the body and the environment. Here, we do not need to distinguish between the two options and take a view that no one approach is better than the other. In line with the ideas of Montero et al. (2019), our focus is, therefore, on "what instruction will elicit the best outcome" (p. 205). Whatever be the instruction, the key requirement is that it allows movements to self-organise in a subconscious or implicit way.

However, directing search through instructional constraints can be problematic for a coach when trying to help learners to acquire complex coordination patterns such as golf swings because it is difficult to know where to tell the learner to focus their attention. Consequently, the golf coach will often need to use questions to guide the discovery and enable the player to find their optimal point of focus. In Case Study 1, we demonstrate how PA worked with Alistair to build his awareness by using rating scales to explore movement solutions and encouraging him to associate the movement pattern with the performance out-come of the trial.

One final point of caution we would offer coaches when considering where to direct attention is that because hitting a golf ball requires the coordination be-tween multiple joints and muscles, the focus of attention should generally be di-rected at promoting the whole of the movement because all the body parts work together to solve the problem. A directed focus on specific body parts has the po-tential to interfere with these natural self-organisation tendencies and could lead to a disruption in the emergent couplings and a freezing of the system of degrees of freedom (Davids et al., 2008). In effect, the search could be directed to an in-formation source that captures the effect of all the performer's muscles working together – one focal point for golf coaches is the head of the golf club. Below we provide an example of how Gallwey (1979) linked auditory information to help develop an awareness of the position of the club head at key points in the swing.

Building Awareness in the Golf Swing

As highlighted in the previous sections, the expert golfer can make compen-satory adjustments to his/her golf swing at a subconscious level. Essential to this process is learning to 'sense' the position of the club head, and for the high handicapper, "it is more important to know where the club head is, not where it should be," (Gallwey, 1979, p. 23) when trying to improve his/her ball-striking ability. As Gallwey articulates:

> The art of control comes from being able to acquire information from your body early enough during the swing so that the body can correct any mis-alignment *before* impact. This correction cannot be made consciously, but [the body] can perform subtle last-minute adjustments below the threshold of conscious awareness if he/[she] is trusted to do so.
>
> *(Gallwey, 1979, p. 131)*

In the *Inner Game of golf*, Gallwey (1979) describes numerous ideas to build aware-ness and promote self-organisation. Concerning the golf swing, he provided two strategies to help create awareness by focussing attention on the club head, which he describes as the 'critical moving object' (p. 22). Gallwey suggested using audi-tory information to create awareness of the kinaesthetic information correspond-ing to the position of the club head during the key phases of the golf swing. For example, Gallwey's (1979) first idea is to say "back" at the moment he felt that the club head was at the top of the backswing and "hit" at ball contact (Figure 3.8). Later, Gallwey refined this two-cadence rhythm to a three-cadence one. Now he added another anchor point at the finish of the follow through. This time, Gall-wey, suggesting using "da-da-da" to verbally couple to the top of the backswing, the contact, and the end of the follow through. By directing the search to the position of the club head he provided an individual-specific 'rhythmic hook or

FIGURE 3.8   Developing awareness using Back-hit (Gallwey, 1979). The golfer develops awareness of the position of his/her club during the swing by calling
out "back" when the club is at the top of the backswing and "hit" when
contact is made with the ball.

metric' to calibrate one's actions (Warren & Verbrugge, 1984). One final point
we would add to this example is that the optimal cadence of the swing often
changes from day to day and we would encourage coaches to work with players
to find their rhythm at the start of every session. In the rest of the chapter, we will
focus on how PA puts the ideas we have discussed so far into practice with his
clients. We start with Alistair before finishing with John – the come-back kid.

Case Study 1: The 25 Handicapper With a Slice

A key tool I use often to build awareness is Scaling, quite simply assigning
a number to where I have directed the golfer's search and experimentation.
Let's look at an example by considering how I built Alistair's awareness of
his own game using this approach.

Background

Alistair is 6 feet 5 inches tall, an ex-rugby player, and 39 years of age.
When Alistair first came to see me his handicap was 25, but that was gen-
erous, to say the least. For the amount of club head speed Alistair produced
with a 7 iron (over 90 mph), the ball was only travelling about 100 yards,
mainly right, and very high. You would expect that a well-struck shot

with that club head speed should result in the ball travelling about 170 yards. I observed that Alistair's club head was extremely open throughout his golf swing, with a cupped left wrist at the top of the golf swing (see Figure 2.4). I informed Alistair that the goal in this session was for him to explore and find a way to get the club face less 'open' throughout the swing and then at impact, but first I wanted to know a little more about his background. After a short conversation, I found out a potential reason for the swing he was producing was a fused right wrist from an old rugby injury which resulted in him having limited mobility. Alistair also thought he was swinging the golf club too fast and that he should slow down. So, we set about exploring Alistair's grip first and foremost using the CLA Principle 4: Repetition without Repetition, to help him find a grip that gave him as much mobility in the wrist as was possible. Initially, I asked Alistair to experiment with different grip positions to find out how that affected his wrist movement. I also used the CLA Principle 2: Constrain to Afford, and told Alistair I was looking to see a grip position that allowed him to rev his left hand as much as he possibly could, just like he was revving a motorbike (the analogy worked as Alistair had ridden a motorbike before). This process took several months of exploration in and outside lessons before Alistair found the best grip that felt comfortable, functional, and allowed a range of motion in his right wrist. Part of the process involved building his awareness using scaling to explore how much Alistair could 'rev the motorbike' during the golf swing and finding out what different degrees of 'revving' did to the resultant strike and ball fight outcome. When setting this up, we first assigned values using a 1–10 scale:

Scale number	Description
1	Alistair's old wrist movement – or using the language Alistair used 'no revving of the motorbike'
5	'a little bit of revving of the motorbike'
10	being 'revving of the motorbike early and hard'

I told Alistair that I would call out a number and he was to try and hit the ball with the goal of matching his wrist action to that number. I called "1" and Alistair picked up his favourite 7 iron and sure enough the same habits emerged and the ball flew about a 100 yards high and right. I then called a "10" on the scale and stood back to see if anything changed. "Wow," Alistair said, "I've never hit a golf ball like that before." What ensued was a shot that hooked left of the target, but with a much lower ball flight that travelled 166 yards! Engaging in this process helped Alistair build awareness of his own actions and after quite a few tries he concluded that number 7 on the scale resulted in the best outcome. In later sessions, when Alistair was more comfortable with the new grip and the 'revving of the motorbike' analogy we addressed Alistair's other initial thought that he was swinging the golf club too fast. We used scaling again in conjunction with the 'revving the motorbike' scaling (where Alistair current number was still around 7) with 1 being a 'very slow swing' and 10 being a 'blur'. I led with a '1 then a 10'. The 1 speed with 7 revving produced a massive hook! The 10 speed with 7 revving produced a high fade. Again, I let Alistair lead and spent the session exploring different numbers. I used probing questions throughout to direct his attention and asked him to report what number he was going for before each shot and then report back afterwards as to whether he had felt like he had hit his numbers. Alistair concluded that a 5 speed and a 6 or 7 revving produced the best results for him that day. The beauty of this experimentation also allowed, almost accidentally, the beginnings of an understanding for Alistair on how to curve the ball flight in different ways. When he revved the motorbike with a slower tempo, the ball hooked, and when there was little to no revving and a fast tempo, the ball sliced.

Alistair's homework throughout this time was to experiment on the golf course (ideally) or if not on the driving range, so that he could build awareness of what each club felt like and what numbers on the scales worked best for each club. At first, it took Alistair a while to build awareness with different clubs and he felt more comfortable with his 7, 8, and 9 iron.

I worked with Alistair for over a year using this process with him coming to see me for two hours once a month. Of course, as Alistair engaged in his practice it brought some interesting observations about the nature of learning. A few months into the process, Alistair came in and he found he was hooking the ball to the left quite severely and was quite confused, given he was still using a 7 on the scale, which had worked brilliantly at the start of the process. I asked him if he had experimented with different numbers on the scale given that 7 wasn't working any more to which he replied, "no I haven't because number 7 has been working so well." Herein lies the problem. I used the following quote from Heraclitus and then put it into a golf context.

> No man ever steps in the same river twice, for it's not the same river and he's not the same man
>
> *(Heraclitus cited by Khan, 2003)*

I followed with, "we are not robots, we change and how we feel changes from day to day, we might have slept in a funny position, been to the gym the day before and feel a little stiffer in the muscles, sat at a desk for extended periods of time compared to the day before. Therefore, our bodies and our emotions will change from day to day, hour to hour and potentially minute to minute!"

Accidentally, I gave a demonstration of this concept to a student, in a playing lesson last week. We were playing a long par 3 and I was hitting a 4 iron, and given that my normal shape of the shot is a fade, I aimed at the left-hand side of the green expecting it to fade it back to the middle. However, the ball ended up slicing to the right of the green. Over a period of a few holes, a similar pattern emerged, with me curving the ball to the right too much. At some point throughout the round (it took me too long by the way), I adapted how I was trying to hit the golf ball, to try and create a feeling in my swing like I was trying to curve it more right to left. What transpired, was a small fade with a ball flight that moved slightly to the right, the shape of shot I was originally looking for. I explained what had happened to my student and explained that:

> For things to remain the same, everything must change
>
> *(Tancredi, no date)*

Essentially, I had to change the feeling in my swing for things to stay the same. Because *'No man ever steps in the same river twice, for it's not the same river and he's not the same man'*. So, for the fade to remain the same, everything must change. Now, of course, I didn't give this whole story chapter and verse in a coaching session, well at least I hope I didn't!

Going back to Alistair's now wild hook, so as 7 on the scale didn't work anymore, we explored different revving numbers in the session and soon a 4 on the scale was working better and led to a straighter ball flight.

In summary, developing awareness in practice, and sometimes in competition, allows the golfer to develop a level of awareness and confidence where he/she is not scared to change things in his golf swing when practising or playing. Getting to this level can only be achieved by experimentation and awareness. At a high handicapper level, I am of the belief that the level of experimentation and awareness should just focus on the tools, that is, the golf clubs, and how to manipulate them in a way that gets the desired outcome. In the next case study, I provide examples of this approach in my work with John, to solve problems he had that are typical of a high handicapper.

Case Study 2: The Come-Back Kid

Background

John is 54-year old New Zealander, who asked me to work with him when in Scotland on a golfing holiday. As it is important to see how someone plays on the course and not just how they hit on the driving range, I took John out for a game of golf. He joined me in a four ball with one of my stable of players and a friend to play the championship course at North Berwick. North Berwick is a historic links course with the Club being formed in 1832 and is "an excellent test of golf" (https://www.northber wickgolfclub.com). For John, this was indeed going to be a real test as he reported that at the age of 54 he had just taken up golf again after not play-ing for 15 years (and then to a handicap in the mid-20s).

On-Course Performance Analysis

Although he started well with a birdie and a bogey, John's true game was soon revealed with a pick-up after hitting a big sliced drive on the fourth. Through-out, he mixed some decent hits with inconsistent quality of contact, especially on his iron shots. At times, he hit good approach shots but lacked touch around the greens. My initial observations were that John was able to strike the ball well, at times, but often 'duffed' shots 20–30 yards due to hitting the ground before the ball. Additionally, most drives were sliced and this lost him distance and often resulted in missed fairways. On the whole, John's putting was ade-quate, although he reported having difficulty judging pace back in NZ.

The Coaching Lesson

As previously emphasised, before we decided what to work on with a player during a coaching session it is important to get an understanding of the player's movement history as well as their golf background. At the beginning of the lesson, I quizzed John about his *Movement* and *Sporting History* as well as his *understanding of* golf. In particular, I wanted to know his concept of what he thought was 'right' in terms of factors such as the contact point, where the ball should be placed in the stance and his under-standing of it, which he had gained from talking to other golfers or from reading and watching videos of top players off the web. John reported that he had just started playing golf again after 20 years and his previous lowest score was a 91. At this stage of his come-back, he had yet to break 100 on his home course in Auckland. He had previously played cricket and when he was much younger, football. Unfortunately, this had resulted in a torn anterior cruciate ligament in his right knee that had resulted in several operations. Additionally, he had suffered rotator cuff injuries because of his cricket and in his more recent role as coach, had regular problems in his lower back from throwing balls at his players. I began to form a picture of the reasons why John's golf swing looked the way it did and why he was experiencing lower back pain after playing golf. Given his injury background and general work habits (heavily desk-based), it was evident that John's mobility was not quite what it was when he was in his 20s! John's swing was overly long with a bent left arm at the top of the swing as a result of adapting round his torn right rotator, which culminated in the lack of mobility. The over swing in turn caused John's spine to go into excessive extension (reverse-tilt in golf speak) and caused tension in John's lower back, mainly from the lack of mobility in the rotator cuff (hence the importance of understanding historical constraints). I took in this information as I built my understanding of John's golf game and added this new knowledge to what I had seen on the course. I asked John to choose a club that he was most comfortable with and hit ten balls while I watched. I filmed this on my iPad, with the aim of sharing my observations with him.

After completing his ten shots, I invited John to watch his swing on the iPad and asked for his observations. He noticed that he was making a very full swing which was leading to inconsistency in where he hit the ground, often before the ball. I pointed out the variation in where he was taking divots and he remarked that some were behind the ball and some were in front. I noted that John had three 'rate limiters' or key factors that were currently acting as a brake on his golf game. The biggest problem was the inconsistency in where he was hitting the ground. "Let's go to work on these factors to start with," I said. "We can then work on your slice."

Coaching Interventions

Rate Limiter 1a: Finding the Optimal Swing Length

As mentioned above John's swing length was impacting the quality of his contact with the ball. As the swing was too long, he had too much 'bad' variability and this explained the inconsistency in the bottom point of the swing. My intervention was framed around repetition without repetition to promote exploration by asking John to hit with different swing lengths to help guide his 'discovery' of the most optimal back swing for him at this stage of his development (Figure 3.9). I asked John to undertake a 'full' (100%) swing and told him this was a '10'. I then asked him to swing a 7 (70%), a 3 (30%), and a 5 (50%). In essence, my goal was to 'reduce the degrees of freedom' (see Chapter 2) and decrease the total amount of

FIGURE 3.9 Creating awareness scales can help the golfer notice differences in their movements. For example, to learn to control the length of the swing, the golfer can be asked to make a full swing which can be categorised as a 10 and then asked to swing a 7, 5, or 3.

variability in the swing by having him swing 'shorter'. I filmed him hitting the balls with this reduced swing. I asked him what he thought and he remarked that the quality of contact immediately improved and that not only was he hitting it more cleanly, but the best swing was a 5 and the distance he hit it was just as far with this swing as when he used his full swing. John related this swing to a 'bunt' in cricket, my reaction was "brilliant, use that analogy as it is relatable to a movement that you have done many thousands of times" (instead of trying to relearn an entirely new movement and therefore potentially speeding up the process of positive change). In effect, John reduced the amount of bad variability (linked mainly to lack of mobility) in the trajectory of the swing which meant he had a better chance of contacting the ball first.

"Where Should I Put the Ball in My Stance?"

Often the direction of my golf lessons emerges as a result of the interactions with the golfer. In this lesson, John asked what was a challenging problem for him, namely "where should I put the ball in my stance?" This led us to a discussion about what a good contact looked like and in particular where the divot created by an iron shot should be in relation to the ball. Interestingly, John thought that the divot should be before contact. This question is, of course, related to the challenge of hitting the ball at the bottom of the swing. The answer is 'it depends' as the golf swing is a dynamic system where fluctuations in the player's intrinsic dynamics will influence the swing. For example, before I became a full-time coach, I (PA) used to travel 400 miles per day in my day job and would arrive on the range on an evening stiff and sore. Consequently, my range of movement was limited, and the low point of my swing was much further back in my stance. As I loosened up, the ball position moved more to the middle of the stance as my movement was more dynamic (See Figure 3.10). Therefore, I developed an awareness task for John to use with his new shortened swing. I posed the challenge to John of hitting ten balls at the same target with a 5 iron, however, with the ball in a different position in the stance each time (i.e. CLA Principle 4: Repetition without Repetition). After finishing the task, I asked John which ball position seemed to give him the most success. John replied "middle to the back of my stance, which is strange because I read a golf magazine that said I should put the ball position more towards my left heel with a 5 iron!" I smiled and replied, "don't believe everything you read John!" We then did this task many times over with different clubs and then at different targets. In the following lesson, we trotted out to the golf course (using CLA Principle 3: RLD and Principle 4: Repetition without Repetition) and created similar tasks but off side hill, downhill, and uphill lies. Varying the task constraints helped John develop and find the best ball position for each of these shots so that he began to understand the implications for ball flight, and in particular, how ball position and the nature of the slope interacted.

FIGURE 3.10 Despite definitive advice in golf books, where to place the ball in the stance 'depends' as the player is a dynamic system. Experimenting with different ball position can help the player find their own optimal solution.

Rate Limiter 2: The Slice and Bending it Like Beckham

Golfers have always been encouraged to have 'swing thoughts' to help them with tempo or rhythm. In terms of helping players change techniques, the coach can share information in the form of analogies, metaphors, or visual cues to help players shape or reshape the golf swing (CLA Principle 2: Constraint to Afford). For example, as mentioned earlier, John had a big slice, especially with his driver. As we discussed in Chapter 1, a potential cause was John's background as a cricketer; John had a more vertical swing that went straight back and straight forward, which was not dissimilar to a cricket batting swing. In contrast, in golf, there is a need for a more rotary swing. I drew on my knowledge of John's background to help me create the idea of a rotary swing in John's head. Given his background as a footballer, I asked John to describe a David Beckham free kick, where he bent the ball over and around the wall to score in the top corner. I told John this was how I wanted the swing to feel. To help him get the idea, I told him we were going to play a game where he got points for hitting the ball through a 'gate' and hitting a target. I placed two alignment rods vertically 2 m apart at a distance of 3 m in front of him. I then lined him up with the left pole and told him he had to hit the flag on the fairway 180 yards away, which was directly behind the left pole, but to do it he had to swerve the ball through the gate – he needed to bend it like Beckham! I said I want you to hit 10 shots and there are 5 points on offer for each shot for a total of 50 points. I then spelt out the scoring system: "You get 2 points for hitting it through the gate and then 1 point if you land it within 20–10 yards right of the flag, 2 points if the ball finished to 0–10 yards right of the flag, and 3 points if the ball finishes left of the flag. Essentially, I wanted to create rewards for the right to left ball flight. John immediately created a more rotary swing and smashed a drive 200 yards to land the ball beyond the flag, but 10 yards to the right. "Wow," I smiled and added, "that's 4 points then". After his 10 shots, John had 35 points and had shaped the ball right to left on every shot. John's face revealed his excitement at the dramatic improvement and said, "I now know how to get rid of my slice and how a good swing feels."

This example provides several key points to note when using a CLA. First, the use of the constraint should only be left in for a short period of time to ensure that the golfer does not become over-reliant on it. Once the player can achieve the task, the constraint should be removed then used intermittently, if at all. For example, in the above example, I removed the pole after 5 goes and had John hit his drives without the pole being present. Interestingly, John reported that he was still trying to hit it through the (now) imaginary gate. Additionally, the scoring constraints to emphasise an outcome (CLA Principle 1: Intentions) are the key to allowing the golfer to self-organise his movements and supersedes any need to describe where the hands or the arms should be at various phases of the swing. Creating a focus on the outcome at the same time as giving the golfer a metaphor (Bend it like Beckham) leads to the golfer creating the movement needed to shape the ball flight to achieve the task goal of scoring as many points as possible. In this case, the solution occurred quickly, but sometimes more exploration is needed and should be encouraged. Questions can also help direct the search for the best solution. Now we move onto another common problem of high handicappers possessed by John: not knowing how to get out of bunkers.

Rate Limiter 3: Trapped in the Sand: The Splat

Given we had made good progress in terms of his driving and iron play, I asked John if he had any other things he wanted to work on when he got back home to New Zealand. John spoke about his inconsistency in getting out of bunkers, so we moved over the short game area. I threw a few balls into the bunker and asked him to hit them out towards the flagstick. John, much to his surprise, hit the first ball close to the pin, however, he badly shanked his second shot, and nearly hit a fellow golfer practising $90°$ to his right. After a hasty apology, John had another go, but his confidence was now completely gone and he tentatively tried to get the ball out without following through and left the ball under the front lip of the bunker. It was clear John was struggling with the same problem that he had with his irons; the place where he hit the sand was too inconsistent with regards to depth, and in relation to the ball, he generally hit the sand too far behind the ball. I needed to check what his concept of a good bunker shot was and asked him whether the club face should be hitting the ball or sand. John replied that he had read that you should hit the ball about 2–3 cm behind the ball and scoop sand and ball by hitting through the sand and under the ball. I asked John some questions and highlighted that his first problem was his concept of where a good contact point should be. I then drew a line in the sand (CLA Principle 2) and placed the ball just in front of the line (target side) and got John to hit a few bunker shots. What was evident, was that John hit the sand a few inches behind the ball. I suggested that this was a basic physics problem and asked him what happened to the force of the club head when it made contact with the sand so far behind the ball. John replied that all of the energy went into the sand and it, therefore, slowed the club head down. I asked where he should make contact then, and he replied that it should make contact closer to the bottom of the ball in order for the club to slide under the ball and transferring more of the energy of the sand to the ball. I nodded, but also highlighted that getting the ball out meant hitting this spot fairly consistently and at the moment he had the same problem in the bunker as was seen in his iron play in terms of his ability to hit a consistent point on the sand. I also noted that the angle of the club head was being delivered into the sand also problematic. To illustrate this point, I asked John to describe the sound that the club had made when he hit the shot. He described it as a digging sound, a thud. I then hit a few balls and asked him to describe the sound I made. He described it as a splat. I then asked John to compare my interaction with the sand

FIGURE 3.11 We would not recommend giving the high handicapper this challenging bunker shot as a starter!

to his. John described how his sound was much deeper and narrower than mine. I explained that the splat sound and compressed sand was achieved by laying the back of the club face 'on' the sand and splatting the sand just before the ball. John had a few goes at making the splat sound with his club before having another go at getting out of the bunker based on his new understanding of what good bunker play should look and sound like. To help focus his attention I drew a line in the sand, placed the ball on the edge of the line and asked him to hit the line. While the results were not immediately perfect, John left with a better understanding of how to get out of bunkers consistently. In his practice, I asked John to first of all work on getting the ball 'in the air' before worrying about distance control.

Taking Changes to the Course

The golf coaching industry, I think has done a superb job of understanding the golf swing and all the intricacies of it, one only has to look at the plethora of information on the golf swing on YouTube to see this. However, the technicalities of the golf swing are only one small piece of the golfing pie. An area that is underutilised, undervalued and not fully understood in the golf coaching industry is taking technical changes made on the range or indoor area and applying them to the golf course, or offering advice on how to apply them on the golf course. Any golf coach worth their salt can get a reasonably abled golfer to hit the ball 'better' on the range, however, can they aid this progression to the golf course? In my opinion this is where we as golf coaches have failed miserably, and I'm (PA) as guilty as the next golf coach in this domain. Crucial here is understanding CLA Principle 3.

RLD

The hard part, taking it to the course, especially if the technical changes have been made out of context from the golf course (i.e. the driving range or indoor golf area). In the case of John, the improvement in the brief time we spent working on his game in Scotland initially failed to transfer when he went back to his home golf course. The confidence he had gained from our work on his driving and iron play was soon gone, and he was at a loss to understand the lower success rate which was far lower than on the golf course when compared to his range session with me or when practising in New Zealand. Luckily, I have experience and a greater knowledge base (in no small part of the other two authors in this book), drawing on the many case studies like John's, therefore, I could 'educate' and reassure John. Many times, I have seen technical changes not transfer to the golf course, here is a more extreme example and the story I told John over the phone also to reassure him:

One winter I had a new client called Frank, Frank was in his mid-40s, physically able, and played lots of sport. With regards to golf, Frank had played on and off for over 30 years. However, now golf was his main passion and he wanted to dedicate more time to improving his game. Frank played at a golf course called The Musselburgh Golf Course (on the outskirts of Edinburgh, Scotland) which is 6,725 yards long and a par 71. Off the tee, Frank hit it about 240 yards, however, like John he had a big slice. Long story short, we fixed Frank's slice, or so we thought....

Over a period of four months (the winter months of November to March), Frank came in for an hourly lesson every two weeks. Due to the constraints of the weather, daylight, and Frank's work schedule, all of these sessions were in an indoor area fitted with Trackman Technology (see picture below). By late February, Frank's slice had completely disappeared and he could regularly hit draws on Trackman right from the start of the session without any input from myself (a reasonable marker for retention). However, John kept coming back to me after each lesson saying he was still slicing on the golf course, despite the success indoors. To begin to understand the problem, I needed to see Frank's behaviour on the golf course. So, in late March we toddled off to the golf course after hitting a few balls indoor to warm up (all nice draws). I took Frank to the 16th hole, which had significant boundaries on it and a good drive was at a premium. All hell broke loose, the nice draws that we had seen just five minutes ago had turned into 30-yard slices! So, what happened? Well, perceptually, for 30 years Frank had seen a hole through his slice, so on the golf course, he aimed to allow for it.

Implicitly, it had become a habit in order to perform functionally (well as functional as you can with a 30-yard slice ☺). So, Frank's body aligned, you guessed it, 30 or 40 yards left of the target, making it impossible to hit a draw! So why could he draw in the indoor area then, but not on the course? Well, in the indoor area, the matt Frank was hitting off was perfectly aligned (straight) to the target which was on a screen about 15 feet in front of him. There was also no other perceptual information such as boundaries, water, trees, or dynamic environmental features such as clouds or wind. Therefore, indoors, I did not see any of the body alignment attuning to the external information that we see in the real environment and once again highlights the importance of considering RLD in coaching!

The story resonated with John, and he asked, "so what did you do next." I replied that we addressed this by using the same scaling (the methods I described earlier with Alexander).

I worked with Frank to assign values to the numbers and we came up with the following scoring system:

Scaling number	Description
1	The old set up aiming 30–40 yards left
10	Aiming at the tree right of the fairway
20	Aiming right of the trees

I added, "I also want you to try and replicate the draw feeling that was working indoor whilst doing this game". I shouted out "1" and sure enough Frank hit a big slice again. I called out 10, and it was a smaller slice this time. Then I asked for a 20, asked him to go extreme, feeling like he was aiming right of the trees. Frank looked at me as if I was crazy, but I was insistent, "try it" I said, "what's the worst that can happen?" I filmed Frank from behind, he hit a perfect draw that started down the middle of the fairway and ended up on the left-hand side of the fairway. When I showed Frank the film, he replied "No way!" he added, "but I'm aiming down the middle of the fairway and it feels like I am aiming miles right!"

Going back to John, he realised that he was having the same problem, as he was still setting up to allow for his slice and the stance was preventing him from drawing the ball. "Ok I get it, I need to start exploring and experimenting where I am aiming on the golf course!" A WhatsApp message with a thumbs up arrived a few weeks later with a short video of John standing square to the target and drawing the ball down the fairway. "Next stop chipping over a bunker from a bare lie!" John quipped.

Summary

The high handicapper's search for a higher level of success is often framed by the search for consistency. However, this is rarely attained and is often lost in the pursuit of the perfect swing with the consequential over-reliance on repeating the same movement in the same place over and over again. This flawed approach is framed on the popular fallacy prevalent in golf and all other sports that we need to build up our 'muscle memory' so we can run off good golf swings at will. In contrast, the most effective golfers are ones who can adapt their golf shots to the needs of the moment. Part of this process is increased awareness gained through significant levels of exploration in their learning and practice. Awareness training can be used effectively by building scales that allow golfers to learn to notice the differences between movements. Starting at the 'extremes' of a scale help this process and often requires exaggeration of the opposite action to the problem. For example, whilst these contrasts can be about the shape or length of a swing, it could also involve manipulating environmental constraints such as hitting off a steep upslope and then a steep downslope. Adding analogies or metaphors to help the golfer create a feel or image of the new action is often a useful strategy. Whenever possible, the golfer should be involved in the creation of these phrases in order so that it has meaning for him/her. A final point is the importance of developing strategies that encourage and promote ownership of the performance where the golfer has the confidence and autonomy to solve golf problems on their own. A key part of this aim is the use of probing questions to find out the golf knowledge of their players to check what they understanding of it, as often engagement with 'golf education' via social media can lead to misunderstandings or an attraction towards solutions that are not optimal for the individual. Pete's conversation with John about where to put the ball in the stance is a good example in the chapter. Given that the coach cannot hit shots for the golfer, the ability to attune to the key affordances of the golf environment becomes essential, and when achieved can enable their exploitation. A nice example would be the golfer who has constantly struggled to hit a short chip onto a raised green from the bottom of the bank. Exploring different strategies may reveal to the player that the most functional solution for them would be to hit the ball into the bank, taking the pace out of the ball and allow it to drop softly onto the green. A final point is that golf is played on the course, so whenever possible, learning should take place there. It is important to remember that the environment they play in will shape the specific abilities they can and will need to develop to improve as a player. To that end, learning on the course, will 'invite' players to develop skills such as a draw, a fade, low, bump and runs, or high fades with lots of spin.

Key Points

- Know the player and the environment
  - Get an understanding of the movement, sporting, and golf history.
  - What are his/her goals?
  - Knowing the player's work-related background is also useful for learning how to communicate your ideas.
  - What is the golf environment of the player?

- • Knowing the golf environment will impact your decision-making as a coach.
- • Understanding golf concepts
  - • Use questions to develop an understanding of the player's concepts of what 'good' looks like.
- • Reduce the degrees of freedom
  - • Simplify the swing by reducing its length.
- • External focus of attention
  - • Cut the line: Decompose briefly before using a waffle ball or real golf ball.
  - • Use targets to shape shots.
- • Use metaphors and analogies
  - • Use task instruction based on the player's background.
    - • "Bend it Like Beckham."
- • Use sound to highlight outcomes
  - • "Splat"

4

SO YOU WANT TO TURN PRO?

Introduction

What does it take to become a professional golfer? What are the key determinants for success? Being able to answer these questions is a basic requirement for any golf coach tasked with preparing a young player for a future career as a professional golfer. In this chapter we will discuss the key factors that need to be considered when coaching a player who is 'close' to turning professional and every session needs to have that goal as a focus. We will consider the issue in terms of what it takes to make one of the major tours: the US PGA Tour or the European Tour. Of course, before one can play on the major tours, players have to pass through qualifying tours. This process is cut-throat and, in some ways, can be viewed as being harder to succeed in than attempting to stay on the major tours. For example, the Web.com qualifying tour, which is the development tour for the US PGA Tour has an incredibly high standard of play. To illustrate how a young golfer who wants to turn pro needs we will focus on what it takes to be successful for a young player attempting to use this tour (and its European equivalent) as a stepping stone. To bring the ideas to life, we will look at the question from Paul's point of view, a Scottish golfer who aims to make it to the European Tour. In this section, Pete will draw upon the learnings he took from his Masters study: "Scottish European Tour Professionals experiences of playing and developing towards the European Tour: Through the lens of a Constraints-led Approach." We will then conclude, by providing specific examples of practice activities that we undertook with "Paul" (as part of a development programme to help him to try and achieve his goal of qualifying for the European Tour). A key principle that underpins all of the ideas in this chapter is that of RLD. As we have discussed earlier in the book, RLD asks the coach to consider the coherence between practice and performance, and at the elite level, ensures that the landscape of affordances available for players to attune to and exploit are present, which is crucial to the likelihood of positive transfer to tournament play. Consequently, the key question we constantly asked ourselves when designing learning tasks was, "does it look and feel like the real thing? Perhaps, you can try the games out, and out of 10, give a score as to how well each activity achieves this goal." Figure 4.1 is a dial we have developed that encourages practitioners to think about the level of representativeness they wish to build into their practices. The 1–10 scale highlights that all activities do not necessarily have to exactly replicate the performance setting; however, we would suggest that the higher the standard of the golfer, the more the practice environment is representativeness of the performance environment, the better. This is so that performers can learn to exploit the landscape of affordances that are present in performance settings.

Given the goal of preparing players for the 'tour', we first considered what skills and abilities we felt that a player would need and compared it to the skills that were already in place. Of course, to do that we wanted to ensure our definition of skill was in line with the one we introduced in Chapter 1. To recap, as defined by Araújo & Davids (2011), the most skilful golfers are the ones that are best 'attuned' or 'adapted' to their environments. Clearly, to become more adapted to specific environments requires players to actually have opportunities to develop the skill sets needed to play in those environments. Consequently, a key role of the coach training a player with the ambition to play on the tour is that he needs to identify the key environmental, task, and organismic constraints

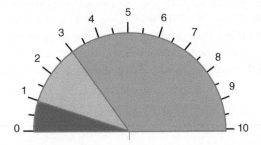

FIGURE 4.1 The representativeness dial. The use of this dial encourages coaches to decide how 'representative' of the performance environment they want the practice environment to be. Using the dials emphasises that coaches can 'turn up' or 'turn down' the level of representativeness of practice within a session. A good guide is to check if the observed behaviour 'looks and feels like the real thing'. Coaches should carefully consider using Red (0–1) or Amber (1–3) Zone tasks where key information sources are missing, and the likelihood is the emergence of perception-action skills that have limited transfer to the performance environment. For the Green Zone (3–10) task, coaches are encouraged to try and move the dial closer to the ten. Often, this would involve creating tasks that create similar emotions and thoughts as in the performance environment not just replicate the information in the environment.

impinging on the performance of tour professionals. Identifying such factors would help ensure that as coaches we can design practice tasks that take place with potential professional golfers in environments that are as 'representative' of the experiences of competition as possible. We begin with an analysis of tour data from a feeder tour and then the PGA tour, and follow that with a discussion of the Scottish amateur golf environment.

Analysis of Tour Data

The web.com Tour

As highlighted above, before making the major tours, golfers have to pass through feeder tours. Here we will focus on the scoring demands of playing on the web.com tour, arguably the most difficult tour to play professionally on. The web.com tour feeds into the US PGA Tour with the top 25 money earners automatically awarded a card for the PGA Tour. Hence, the need to perform consistently well is paramount and every shot counts. For example, in 2018, 34 players on the web.com tour averaged under 70 per round, with a further 71 players under 72. These numbers need to be considered in the context that only the top 65 players (and ties) at the end of day 2 in a web.com qualify for the final two days. An analysis of the final scores in 2018 shows that simply qualifying for the final two days of tournaments requires, on average, an under par-score (−0.45) with a range of −5 to +3. To actually win the tournament, you need to score −16.7 with a range of −7 to −26; 2019 is tracking in a similar way. Table 4.1 below shows current winning scores and the score needed to make the cut at the time of writing. Clearly, golf at the highest levels requires significant levels of skill as well as the mental skills to thrive in such a demanding, pressure-filled environment.

TABLE 4.1 Web.com Score for 2019 (up to 16th May 2019)

Tournament (2019)	Winner & score		Making the cut
January 13–16: The Bahamas Great Exuma Classic	Zecheng Dou	−18	Even
January 20–23: The Bahamas Great Abaco Classic	Raphael Campos	−7	+2
January 31–February 3: Country Club de Bogota Champ.	Mark Anderson	−17	−1
February 7–10: Panama Championship	Michael Gligic	−8	+3
February 14–17: Lecom Suncoast Classic	Mark Hubbard	−26	−5
March 21–24: Chitimacha Louisiana Open	Vince Colvello	−19	−2
March 28–31: Savannah Golf Championship	Dan McCarthy	−16	−2
April 18–21: Robert Jones Golf Trail Champ.	Lanto Griffin	−15	Even
April 25–28: Dormie Network Classic	X. Zhang	−26	−3
May 2–5: Nashville Golf Open	R. Shelton	−15	+2
May 9–12: KC Golf Classic	Nelson Ledesma	−11	+1

The PGA Tour Data

A useful tool for the golf coach looking to develop a deeper understanding of the pro golf environment is the accessible comprehensive database of statistics. For example, Albright (2017) found that functional performance on the PGA Tour, when measured by prize money earned, was significantly affected by how far the PGA Tour players drove the ball off the tee. Perhaps the most comprehensive set of data is the ProGolf Synopsis of the 2018 PGA season (Hunt, 2018). This data moves beyond the useful, but often limited, information available in traditional statistics such as fairways and greens hit in regulation, up and downs made, and putts per round. As Hunt highlights, the aim when using the data is:

> to analyse the numbers, determine a range of probability and interpret how to use the findings to better our golf game…[and]… quantify aspects of the game that influence a golfer's score and being able to prioritize them in the order of the greatest influence.
>
> *(p. 7)*

As well as providing a detailed summary of every player on the tour, Hunt provides summary statistics that demonstrate the standard expected on the tour and in effect 'what our golf [PGA tour golf] requires'. Below we provide a summary of the key findings (Table 4.2).

From Amateur to Pro: Key Issues

To find out what golfers thought were the key issues and to identify the potential barriers and needs of prospective tour players, Pete interviewed seven former and current Scottish European Tour golf professionals who had between 2 and 10 years tour experience. Two of the golfers were world-class elite and three were successful elites, as they had experienced occasional success at the top level. The remaining two were defined as competitive elites who have had limited to no success at this level, although they had competed at the highest level. An analysis of the interview provided a unique insight into the individual experiences of each professional golfer during their progression to, and their experiences whilst on, the European Tour. Perhaps the most important point was that Scottish courses require a different style of play than the major tour courses and, therefore, the skill sets developed on these courses often make it difficult for players to adapt. For example, because most Scottish Elite Amateur courses tend to be short and links courses, they are often set up with punitive rough and accuracy is rewarded at the expense of distance when hitting off the tee. Consequently, the need to play driver off the tee is not as great as what is seen in the data above on the main professional tours, which means the golf course shaped their behaviour with the driver, that is, short and straight. One of the players in

TABLE 4.2 Key findings of the PGA tour data analytics

General

1 The average Adjusted Score per Round on Tour in the 2017–2018 season was 70.874 strokes. The average Tour player that qualified statistically also averages roughly 25 events a year. At 70.874 strokes per round, the projected earnings per event would be $74,503.

2 The average course on the PGA Tour is about 7,200 yards. Thus, if a golfer is playing a 6,000-yard course they will likely not go through a round where they hit a 175–225-yard approach shot.

3 True consistency in golf is largely a myth. Great golfers still hit bad shots!

4 25-yard differences in approach shots represents a '2-club difference' (example: 7 iron versus a 5 iron) and is closely linked to expected scores.

5 Good players develop a 'shot cone' with their ball striking. Being able to land balls in a 'shot cone' is because the player has a stock shot that has a consistent ball flight chance (i.e., a left-to-right or right-to-left curvature). This means that when they miss their target, they miss in one direction rather than spraying the ball all over the course.

6 To identify the likely contenders in an event before the weekend play begins, you will likely need to look at all golfers that are within three shots of the lead going into Saturday.

7 The first 6 holes of a round of golf are the most critical. When divided into 6-hole segments, it found that Tour winners gained the most strokes on holes 1–6, 19–24, 37–42, and 55–61. Those are the first six holes of each round.

8 The lowest rounds in a tournament almost exclusively occur in the first and second rounds.

9 Effective golf strategy tends to be more offensive than defensive-minded.

Driving

10 Golfers consistently shoot lower scores when choosing to go for it versus laying up off the tee. The players that hit driver have substantially lower scores, but they hit a much higher percentage of fairways using the driver off the tee than they did using a 3-wood.

11 Club head speed hitting a driver is one of the most crucial measurements on Tour as it has a strong correlation to a player's potential. Higher club head speed golfers can not only hit it further off the tee, but also allow them to hit less club on approach shots, and they are typically the best players out of the rough.

12 Even the best players in the world miss the shot cone from time-to-time; but not by much!

13 Tour players tend to hit their driver just as straight as their 3 wood. The modern driver has a club head that is nearly three times larger than the modern 3 wood. This means less forgiveness and on holes where the landing area is nearly the same size for a 3 wood or driver off the tee, the forgiveness helps the golfer find the fairway more often in those situations.

14 There is a strong correlation between driving distance and birdie putt length. The longer you are the shorter the putts.

15 The longest hitters on Tour are typically the best players on the par-5.

Iron play

16 Inside 150-yards most Tour players are firing at the flag quite often if they have a decent lie.
17 Outside 150-yards the strategies can vary and there is nothing in the research that shows any significant correlation to performance on a macro level.
18 Iron shots into greens can be broken down into four zones. The Green Zone includes shots between 75–125 yards. Yellow Zone shots are 125–175 yards. The two most important Zones for tour golfers are the Red and Yellow Zone. The Red Zone (175–225 yards) has the strongest correlation to Adjusted Scoring Average on Tour and has the second-greatest number of attempts per round with an average of 3.7 attempts per round. The Yellow Zone has the lowest correlation to score.

Short game

19 Shots from 10–20 yards and are adjusted for the schedule of courses played by the golfer. This metric has the strongest correlation to Strokes Gained – Around the Green.
20 The wedge game is overvalued by golfers on all skill levels. The small variance and lack of frequency of wedge shots on Tour make wedge performance inconsequential.

Putting

21 The best putters generally putt the best from 5 to 15 feet.
22 Golfers are much more likely to make uphill putts than downhill putts.
23 The more difficult the greens are to putt on, the more it gives good putters who are poor ball-strikers a better shot at contending at the event.
24 The average make percentage on putts from 15 to 20 feet is about 18%.
25 Putting accounts for roughly 30% of the golfer's score when we remove those putts inside 3 feet (tour pros make 99.3% of putts from inside 3 feet).
26 No matter how much a golfer practices or how great they become with the putter, there has been no evidence of a player that can consistently make a higher percentage of putts outside 20 feet for a long length of time.
27 Putting that influences performance (inside 20 feet but greater than 3 feet) is roughly 15%–20% of the game.
28 The shorter, but more accurate golfer is less likely to have those tee shots that miss the fairway by a larger margin and when they miss the green in regulation; they are likely to have shorter up-and-down opportunities on average than the bomber.

the study highlighted the differences in the golf course from the European Tour to Scottish Golf Courses:

> The courses are completely different (on tour)…just totally different, you don't play on the courses we were brought up on, really they're completely different courses.

Similarly, the features of most Scottish courses (wind and greens that are not heavily protected by hazards) invite a low ball flight, with the bump and run a favourite solution when attacking greens. This important point was emphasised by a European Tour player in the study:

> I think it's the style of golf that's played in Scotland, compared to the type of golf that's played on tour....I think the big thing, in the amateur game, the style of golf is not the same as the style of golf you play as a pro.
>
> *(Arnott, 2019)*

A feature of European tour golf that might be presumed to be a positive factor, but actually works in the opposite direction is the availability of top-class practice facilities with the accompanying unlimited supply of decent balls. Players reported that this often led to them over-practising; however, they found that practice on the range wasn't transferring to the course. Essentially, in line with the discussion we had in the Introduction, the skills developed did not transfer effectively. Hence, they found that they needed to actually practice on the course so they could learn to attune to the affordances of the course. A key point for a tour golfer who is faced with playing a wide range of courses across continents is the need to be much more adaptable than when playing on more homogenous Scottish courses. Indeed 5 out of the 7 golfers interviewed, received their biggest pay cheque in professional golf in the UK or Ireland on golf courses that were very similar to the ones they played on during their development. A final point about playing well on tour, was the need to be able to play functional (scoring) golf when not playing well or even when playing badly. In these situations, they talked about learning to play the percentages to grind out a score and having more than one solution to hitting a golf ball. Indeed, one player said he won an event on tour without his A-game.

> The time I won in... I wasn't in a great (form), even during the tournament I wasn't that great, but I played functional, you know I knew where I was going and just kind of played to my strength. So there has been that I've won when I'm not playing that great ... so that week I just aimed to the left and I sliced it back in play. And it's a shot I don't particularly like, it's a low slice as well, not a shot I like but it was a shot that worked. Basically, it's not going the other way, so that's what I did.
>
> *(Arnott, 2019)*

Winning when your 'A' game is missing will be discussed in more depth in the next chapter.

A final point is that for the tour golfer, coming back to Scotland between tournaments produced some significant problems for practice. To demonstrate how I (PA) implement a CLA in my coaching with a player at this stage of their career, I will walk you through the processes I adopt with any golfer. Specifically, I will provide examples of my work with 'Paul' to redesign his practice and competition schedule and give him the best chance of achieving his goal. I will first introduce Paul and highlight his current status, including a summary of his golfing history and how this has shaped his current strengths and weaknesses. I will then highlight how this initial assessment informed the practice design.

Paul: A Case Study of a Scottish Mini Tour Player

Introduction

In 2016, I was approached by Paul who was a top amateur golfer who asked me to help him achieve his goal of qualifying for the European Tour. So, in terms of helping Paul achieve his goal, I needed to take into consideration his golfing background and consider why Scottish amateur golfers were not making successful transitions and come up with a practice and competition strategy to give them the best chance of success.

Paul is 6 feet 2 inches tall (188 cm) and weighed 16 stone (101 kg). He grew up in Scotland, playing multiple sports including football, tennis, and basketball as a child and took up golf 'seriously' at 11 years of age. He became a member of a local club near his home and worked with a highly respected 'technical' coach. However, in comparison to his peers, Paul was a late developer and by 17, was 'only' playing off a 4 handicap. The best 17-year olds are typically playing off plus handicaps. However, by 23, he was off +4 and representing Scotland as an amateur. Paul was currently playing and practising at his local course and competing as an amateur. His home club course is a typical Scottish links course, that is, one that is coastal and consequently the surface is generally undulating and sand-based with long rough. Like many links courses, Paul's home course is short at 6,200 yards and has small greens with an overall par of 71. As the course is short, those responsible for its presentation set up the course to have narrow fairways with significantly punishing rough. Hence, accuracy rather than distance is rewarded off the tee.

The First Meeting

At the time of our first meeting, Paul began by stating that his reason for coming to see me was that he felt I could help him achieve his goal of playing on the European Tour. Specifically, he felt the main areas where I could contribute was in practice design and he was particularly keen that I coach him ON the course.

Practice for Paul, at this point, was mainly solo on a range with a focus on technique, although he also played some games for money, but these were mainly with players of lower ability than him. In summer, Paul used all his leave to play in up to 20 tournaments per year. After careful consideration of the financial implications, Paul decided to turn professional, meaning he could completely devote his time to achieving his ambition. We agreed that a four-year plan would be our timeline, as data shows that most golfers who 'make it' to the European

Tour after turning Professional, do so within that time period. This gave us free rein to design the optimal practice and performance programme.

Evaluating Paul's Strengths and Weaknesses

The first stage of putting together a development plan involved finding out as much about Paul and his golf as I could. I drilled down into his performance using shotshole.com (a statistical package), took a dive deeper into his stats from competitive rounds, interviewed him, and then, in order to triangulate what I had learnt so far, I watched him play in competitive situations. For me, the most important part of this process was watching him play as it enabled me to check whether the data shown and Paul's statements were actually a true reflection of what was happening on the course. Additionally, watching Paul play allowed me to develop a much deeper understanding of his game in relation to key moments or specific situations he encounters that are not revealed by the data on paper. A good example of this was in the first year I worked with him when I followed him round at a Mini-Tour event. A key eye-opener for me was in the last round. Paul came tied 8th and shot 67 that day. He played well, but there were several shots that Paul 'got away with' during the round, in particular, two tee shots and a long iron shot, in particular, that just missed hazards by feet. I noticed a pattern to all of these shots, which were all right to left shots at an angle. Whilst, this shot matched Paul's consistent fade, on these particular shots his body was even more open (pointing left) and the miss was a two miss, either a straight pull left or over fade (slice) right. I wanted to explore this more with Paul and after the round we sat down with a beer and talked it through.

After complimenting him on his round and all the good shots he had played and congratulating him on his finish position, I described the three errant shots and we discussed how they were all at left to right angle. Paul took a few minutes to reflect.....

PAUL: Aha, it is linked to the bay I practice in at my local range. My bay' is the furthest left and it requires me to hit out to the right. I feel really comfortable hitting from there. However, the bay I get my golf swing lessons in, which is at the same range, is the furthest right bay and requires me to aim left, I hate that bay.....

PETE: Interesting, guess where more of your training is going to be from now on?" I said with a smile!

Pulling It All Together

After watching Paul play and considering the data, we sat down to discuss what I had seen and to get his input as well. I see programme design as a joint process where we co-create the programme, so we systematically worked through all aspects of his practice and his game, including his hitting skills; mental skills (concentration, emotional management; confidence, pre-shot routines); physical skills, and his course management skills.

The initial conversation was about practice. Paul highlighted that he loves competing against other players in training and adding consequences such as playing games for cash; games help him concentrate better as he enjoys feeling the 'pressure' it creates. He grew up learning by playing more than hitting balls at the range and he reports that this means that he loves the competitive element of golf but often finds that he gets bored when on the range. He gets easily distracted and 'switches off' especially when it is an 'easy shot', which is often the case when practising a golf swing on a mat to an unspecified target. Our discussions revealed that if you give Paul a target score to hit, or a difficult shot he focuses much harder and has a much more successful outcome relative to the difficulty of the shot. I asked if he ever switched off in tournaments when it was an 'easy' shot and he reported, that he had a habit of doing it, often at critical periods. He gave me a good example, reporting that recently he was leading in a mini tour Professional Golf event by two shots going into 18th hole on the 3rd round and the group in front need a ruling and he had to wait for nearly 40 minutes on the tee. The tee shot was a relatively easy one, but Paul reported that he was so annoyed and distracted with the delay he made a really poor swing and ended up making a treble bogey (on a fairly easy hole). The next day he eventually finished tied for 8th and was three shots off the winning score. "Those *%&#$* three shots" he laughed! With prize money being notoriously top-heavy on these tours (see above), the difference between 8th and top three cost him a lot of money.

We then moved on to talk about Paul's play in tournaments in the context of his upbringing and how this had shaped his current skill set. We started on the tee and agreed that whilst Paul just about hits the ball far enough and straight enough with his driver to play on Tour with a swing speed of 108–110 mph (tour average is 113 mph); this would still mean that he would need to hit more mid-irons into the greens. As Scottish courses are short, his current hitting distance means he is only left with relatively short iron shots into the greens and unsurprisingly he is good from 100 yards and in. On the minus side, Paul was rarely hitting mid to long irons into greens and, therefore, it is no surprise that this area of his game is a weakness. The small greens on Scottish courses have also 'shaped' Paul's strengths as the need for accuracy is at a premium, whilst there will be more probability of Paul missing greens. Playing on Scottish courses has therefore offered Paul multiple opportunities to improve his chipping around the greens in varying lies. Consequently, Paul's short game is a strength. In summary, Paul's action capabilities have been shaped by the environment he has developed in with accuracy over length being a strength off the tee and his short game being top class. However, when Paul is not completely accurate with approach shots to the small greens then the golf course asks him to hit lots of chip shots from varying lies (Figure 4.2).

FIGURE 4.2 Golfers' skills emerge as a function of the courses they play on. For example, the bump and run is a shot for many Scottish golfers. (Picture courtesy of Remco Polman).

By the end of the meeting, we agreed that Paul's training environment was not conducive to helping him 'step up' to the mini tour golf and then the bigger goal of playing on the European Tour. Specifically, the golf courses he was training and competing on were too short and the added length of tour courses meant that Paul would need to develop the ability to hit the ball much further off the tee. Additionally, due to the fact that there will be a significant increase in the number of shots that Paul would need to make from the "Yellow" and "Red" Zone of 175-22 yards (see Table 4.3 below), we wanted to create on and off-course activities where this was the focus. Our general principle was to attempt to make practice as representative of the tour demands as possible; so whenever possible we included individual, task, and environmental constraints that were commensurate with tour courses. The goal of creating highly representative practice meant that as often as possible, we wanted Paul to be hitting his long irons on the course so that he could learn to hit from side hill, downhill, and uphill lies, from different grasses (fairway, light rough, heavy rough), with different winds, and different conditions (e.g., playing in the wet with moisture on the ball). We wanted him to work out the best 'percentage shots' with a target to hit. Finally, we wanted him to develop his depth perception (downhill to a flag, downhill to a green). In fact, we wanted him to have to hit all the shots you don't get on a range. We also wanted to prepare Paul for 'parkland' courses (rather than links) as the ball reacts differently when it hits the ground. On a links course you can generally run the ball into the green from everywhere, whereas, on the typical Parkland courses found on the tour

TABLE 4.3 The average number of approach shots in the green, yellow and red zones and best and average distance from the hole on the PGA tour

Zone	Distances	Shots per round (mean)	Average distance to the hole from the middle-range of zone (mean)
Green	75–125 (68.58–114 m)	2.2	Best:16 feet (4.88 m) Average: 20 feet (6.1 m)
Yellow	125–175 (114–160 m)	5.1	Best: 20 feet (6.1 m) Average: 27 feet (8.2 m)
Red	175–225 (160–205 m)	3.7	Average: 32.4 feet (from 180-feet; 36 feet (10.97 m) from 200 yards and 40.5 (12.35 m) feet from 225 yards)

there is more of a need to be able to fly the ball 'through the air' to carry it onto the green and stop it, as sometimes there are hazards at the front of greens or the greens are raised negating a run shot into the green.

Training Goals

So what abilities do we want to Paul to develop to enable his successful transition to the professional ranks? We prioritised the following areas of his game:

1 Practice: Making every shot count
2 Providing opportunities to learn to play on Long Parkland courses
3 Making the cut and playing 72 holes in four days
4 Hitting long/mid irons into the green.
5 Starting fast: The Six-Hole Challenge

Goal 1: Making Every Shot Count

A key goal that we set to underpin every aspect of Paul's programme was to ensure that every moment spent during training mattered. We therefore removed context-less hitting and drills which Paul had reported led to him losing concentration, replacing them with games which had an outcome focus and consequences. In the games discussed below, the outcome score is always the focus and ensures that Paul is 'striving' (end-directed) to achieve a goal. The aim was to simulate as closely as possible the dynamic nature of performing on tour, and therefore, create similar intentions, thoughts, emotions, and types of shots needed to play on tour. We therefore designed games that tested his weaknesses and used strategies such as adapting courses to simulate tour course; set up games where he played for cash against players who were better than him; simulated phases of tournaments and creating challenging games with different levels using similar principles to those used in computer game design.

Goal 2: Providing Opportunities to Learn to Play on Long Parkland Courses

The task was to help Paul become attuned to the requirements of tour courses. So, quite simply the first intervention required Paul to practice by playing on golf courses more representative of tour golf. In Scotland there are only about four golf courses (out of nearly 600) that are similar to Tour Golf Courses in that they are over 7,200 yards long and parkland; three of these golf courses are generally too expensive or too busy. Therefore, we chose to use The Duke's golf course at St. Andrews. The advantage of this course was that at 7,512 yards long off the back tees it is nearly 150 yards longer than the tour average. An additional feature, which we particularly liked was that that there is the choice of four different tee boxes which enabled us to carefully tailor our sessions to adjust the level of challenge depending on Paul's progress and, significantly, as it is in Scotland, the weather conditions. (Note the link to matching task demands to current skill level we first introduced when talking about how to use CLA to coach beginners in Chapter 2). Quite simply, playing on this golf course would help Paul to learn how to score and play the shots necessary on a tour style golf course. Obviously, the environmental constraints associated with playing and practising in the winter in Scotland play a role here. As the ball does not go as far in the colder conditions. The differences of temperature are significant and Titleist say you'll lose about 1.5% of distance for every 20 degrees of air temperature drop (see here for more details: https://www.weatherworksinc.com/weather-golf-ball-distance). Having to wear more clothing in order to stay warm would also lead to a loss of distance, and when we tested Paul in temperatures around freezing, the extra layers of clothing he had to wear to stay warm led to a considerable swing speed drop from 108/110 mph to 102/103 mph. The greens at The Dukes course are also not of a similar pace or texture to those Paul would generally be facing on tour (running about 7/8 on the stimpmeter, where tour greens are generally 11–13) making the transfer of putting skills more challenging.

As a consequence of the cumulative effect of all of these constraints, asking Paul to play off tour tees in the winter was a tough ask (7,500 yards in cold wet conditions becomes a lot longer relative to 7,500 yards in warm, dry conditions). Therefore, as a result of a fair bit of trial and error, we worked out that the blue tees were the most appropriate to train on in winter (except for all par 3s where they are black), whilst in summer, the black tees were the most appropriate (see Figure 4.3) for distances off each tee. Whilst blue tees generally fitted Paul's needs best in winter and black tees in summer, we also developed games where we shifted across all the tee blocks. One game we regularly used was Snakes and Ladders where the result on a hole determined which tee you playoff on the next hole. For example, a par score would mean hitting off the same tee box, a birdie or eagle meant to move back one or two tee boxes, bogey or double bogey meant to go forward one or two tee boxes. Note here that we decreased or increased

The Duke's

HOLE	1	2	3	4	5	6	7	8	9	OUT		10	11	12	13	14	15	16	17	18	IN	TOT	HCP	NET
	Highland	Drumcarrow	Denhead	Roundel	Beeches	Badgers	Denbrae	Fair Dunt	Craigtoun			Burn Brig	Windbank	Double Dyke	Braw View	Well	Seeding	Melville	Strath	Ice House				
BLACK	528	451	171	433	374	596	513	250	417	3733		448	640	224	424	472	453	231	429	458	3779	7512		
BLUE	499	447	159	401	343	567	470	194	396	3476		426	613	209	405	442	423	213	409	386	3526	7002		
WHITE	479	437	152	375	328	525	435	175	374	3280		400	552	189	386	408	393	188	386	368	3270	6550		
GREEN	473	418	146	347	299	489	406	152	351	3081		369	501	178	363	377	372	163	362	364	3049	6130		
RED	416	294	129	318	277	406	337	121	283	2581		299	453	131	338	313	315	138	338	310	2635	5216		
STROKE	10	6	18	14	12	4	8	16	2			5	1	17	11	13	3	15	7	9				
PAR	5	4	3	4	4	5	4	3	4	36		4	5	3	4	4	4	3	4	4	35	71		

+/-

DATE: COMPETITION:_____ PLAYERS SIGNATURE:_____

PLAYER:_____ HCP _____ MARKERS SIGNATURE:_____

PLAY THE TEE TO SUIT YOUR GAME.	Tee	Red	Green	White	Blue	Black
	Slope - Rating	118 - 70.6	130 - 70.8	134 - 72.7	137 - 74.8	142 - 77.1

FIGURE 4.3 The scorecard for the Dukes course showing distances and pars for four different tee positions.

the level of difficulty based on performance not as an attempt to punish Paul, but to challenge him and encourage him to embrace more difficult situations. A variation of this game was to start at the red tees and see how far you can get back, or start on the black tees and try and stay there. Whenever possible, we got Paul playing against golfers slightly better than him and had them play for money, with the winner as the one hitting from the furthest back tees with the lowest score after 18 holes.

Scorecard for the Dukes course showing distances and pars for four different tee positions.

Playing on The Dukes course provides Paul with the most 'representative' practice possible out of season and when Paul could not get out of Scotland for warm-weather training. We expected that Paul would improve his distance off the tee, but most importantly, we hoped to see an improvement in his long/ mid-iron play. As mentioned earlier, given the lack of transfer in skill Paul experienced when he went from range practice to the course, we wanted as many of these shots as possible to be played in context, with random lies, slopes, and distances, meaning that each time Paul practised these skills, he had a different problem to solve. Of course, we were not expecting an instant improvement and statistically it was obvious he would not be hitting every green and honing his short game skills which were work in progress, but, most significantly, one that was taking place in the 'right' workplace.

Goal 3: Making the Cut and 72 Holes in Four Days

As per the aims of this chapter, Paul was trying to qualify for the Challenge Tour and, ultimately, the European Tours, where the tournament consists of four rounds over four days. Whilst in amateur golf, Paul was used to playing 72-hole tournaments, many of them over a weekend (36 holes a day); therefore, the pace of these tournaments was more 'frantic' than the pace of Tour golf. Hence, one of our goals was getting Paul accustomed to playing one round a day in a tournament and gain an appreciation of the rhythm of play that goes with it. However, to qualify for the last two rounds, he must make the cut which takes place after the second. Here. Only the top 60 players plus ties can qualify from a field of 130–150 golfers. Making the cut, therefore, becomes crucial to making money on the tour and learning to deal with the pressures that it brings which was something we wanted to help Paul develop. To work out what he would need to score in order to make the second round cut score and ultimately win the event, I asked some European Tour Players who had played The Duke's what the winning score and the two round cut would be on the Duke's golf course if a European Tour Event was played there. The general consensus was that somewhere around −10 to −14 for four rounds of golf would be the winning score and level par-to +3 would be the marker for the two-round cut. Weather conditions would obviously be an important factor that may alter these scores. For each simulated tournament we had Paul 'play' in, we would agree on a fair marker for the two-round cut and the winning score on any particular day he played the course. Brooks Koepka (World number one at the time of writing this book) alluded to this with regards to PGA Tour Monday Qualifiers, where you have one round to qualify, versus his experience of playing on the Challenge Tour as a newly turned professional:

> You need to go out and go play four days. If I went and go and tried to chase Monday qualifiers, I might get in four of them (PGA Tour events in a season). Monday qualifiers are hard. You've got to shoot 65 or sometimes even lower. You're not going to be able to do that every week...I'm pretty sure the best players out here (on the PGA Tour), even if they went to go chase Mondays they are not going to get in many events. You go play four days, learn how to handle yourself in tournament conditions, and it's a lot different than firing at a flag for 18 holes. You got to put up a score each day. I think it's the best route (mini-tours). You got to find a place you can play four days and really build your game. You'll find out who you are pretty quickly.
>
> (Koepka, 2019)

Before every 'tournament', we agreed on some negative consequences to make it more real and decided that if Paul missed the two-round cut, he had to simulate what would really happen if he were at a tournament. For example, as he would not have access to a golf course his only option to practice would be to hit on the range. The thought of this would mean him having to make a three-hour round trip to just hit golf balls which, as previously described, he didn't particularly enjoy doing as it was an extremely unappealing outcome for him; he would really much rather focus his mind in attempting to 'qualify' for the final two days. However, we also added in a positive consequence that if Paul made the cut and stayed under par for the tournament, he would be rewarded with a bonus. During these last two rounds Paul and I interacted via WhatsApp with Paul posting his simulated Tournament scores up after every round. At the same time, I posted the 'scores' of his opponents by utilising data from previous tournaments. This gave Paul context and allowed us to simulate where he was on the leader board to create even more context to his play. Paul really enjoyed these 'tournaments' and reflected that it created thoughts and feeling just like those he experienced in 'real' tournaments; one of our key goals in creating representative learning tasks.

Goal Four: Hitting Long/Mid Irons into the Green

Over the winter, we created various on-course and on-range (when the weather is poor or Paul is constrained by time) to sharpen Paul's long game. We specifically created training environments for when circumstances meant Paul couldn't play on The Dukes course (three hours of total travel to and fro) by adapting playing at his home course (6,200 yards). As stated before, we designed and adapted the training around the key behaviours that we were trying to promote within the constraints of the training environment, specifically, driving and long/mid irons.

Activity 1: The Home Run

Whilst The Dukes course met our aims for the first two goals of providing Paul with opportunities to earn to play on Long Parkland courses and, therefore, by default, hitting lots of long/mid irons into well-protected greens, regular access to The Dukes course was often challenging due to logistical issues such as the need to put aside the whole day to travel and play at St. Andrews. Consequently, we needed to create other opportunities for Paul to practice long-to-mid-iron shots into 'real' greens when missing mattered. The solution we came up with revolved round turning Paul's home course into a 'Tour Course' (see Figure 4.4). This required a fair bit of creativity as it is only 6,200 yards long and we wanted to turn it into a 7,300-yard course. Impossible, we hear you say! Well, here is how we did it. The first thing we needed to do was find 1,100 yards. This was actually easier than you would think and simply involved moving the tee shot back on selected par 4s and 5s to create the necessity of hitting a longer second shot on par fours and longer second and third shots (if required) on the par fives. When we had Paul play this game we also added in some additional consequence via the manipulation of task constraints, if he missed his standard distance for his drive.

Competition:												Please indicate which tee used	
DATE		TIME		COMPUTER NO.				Handicap	Strokes Rec'd		SSS 70		
Player A											SSS 69		
Player B											SSS 72		
Marker's Score	Hole	White Tees	Par	Yellow Tees	Stroke Index	Score		Nett Score	W = + L = - H = 0		Red Tees	Par	Stroke Index
						A	B						
100	1	493	5 4	425	10						412	5	7
100	2	363	4	355	6						334	4	9
100	3	326	4	326	14						317	4	11
100	4	388	4	380	4						369	4	3
	5	172	3	159	16						150	3	17
100	6	351	4	326	2						326	4	5
	7	192	3	179	8						168	3	15
100	8	477	5	476	18						454	5	1
100	9	353	4	327	12						303	4	13
700	OUT	3115	36 35	2953							2833	36	
100	10	367	4	355	9						307	4	6
	11	150	3	134	17						122	3	16
100	12	516	5	498	7						490	5	2
	13	205	3	192	1						191	3	12
100	14	357	4	349	13						267	4	14
	15	387	4	380	5						362	4	8
	16	181	3	177	15						151	3	18
	17	452	4	449	3						438	5	4
100	18	500	5 4	488	11						398	5	10
400	IN	3115	35 34	3022							2726	36	
700	OUT	3115	36 35	2953							2833	36	
1100	TOTAL	6230	71 69	5975							5559	72	
STABLEFORD POINTS OR PAR RESULT			HANDICAP						Holes Won.............				
			NETT						Holes Lost.............				
©PremierPlan 01923 711771									Result.....................				
Marker's Signature........				Player's Signature									

FIGURE 4.4 Paul's amended scorecard for the home course with distance adjustment for holes circled. Once Paul had hit off the tee his ball was moved 100 yards back towards the tee to play his second shot.

For example, a drive that was 10 yards down was adjusted back 90 yards, not the standard 80, and one that was 20 yards down or more was moved back 100 yards and had to be played from the rough. Paul's goal was to play the course in par or better, and when he achieved this, we added an extra 100 yards onto the course length. A further task constraint we added to make sure Paul hit 'high' shots into green as required on well-protected tour courses. We did this by penalising him if he bounced the ball up onto the green. Consequently, any shot that ended up landing short of the green had to be played from there was alternatively moved back to the place it first bounced or dropped into any available greenside bunker. This was the constraint that had the most influence on Paul's play and gave him the most challenge. Adapting his flight shape took a lot of time and lots of exploration and accompanying 'error' as he searched for the best ball position, the best club, and the right swing to create a spin on the ball to hold the green. While this sometimes frustrated Paul, and he began to question its worth at times, given the course didn't require this type of shot, he persevered and eventually added this new string to his bow and increased his adaptability in tournaments. Here we see an example of the coach employing Principle 2 (Constrain to Afford) in the practice design process. By designing-in task constraints (rule changes and tee positions) he shapes the affordance landscape and, therefore, invites the desired movement solutions from Paul. Further examples of applying this principle are provided in the remainder of this chapter.

Paul's amended scorecard for the home course with distance adjustment for holes circled. Once Paul had hit off the tee, his ball was moved 100 yards back towards the tee so he could play his second shot.

Activity 2. On Course Practice (The Next Level Game)

The Next Level game (see Figure 4.5) is built around the goal of 'getting to the next level', where the level of difficulty changes from hole to hole depending on performance. In the context of Paul's development, we used the idea to work on his mid-long iron play. If played solo, this game is a good one to play if the course

Level
Level 1 –150 yards (137 metres)
Level 2 –160 yards (146 metres)
Level 3 –170 yards (155 metres)
Level 4 –180 yards (165 metres)
Level 5 –190 yards (174 metres)

FIGURE 4.5 The Next Level Game. Level 1 requires the player to play 3 balls from 150 yards to completion (sinking the putts). The combined score determines if the player moves levels, stays where he/she is, or moves closer to the hole. The game is completed when the player achieves a par on Level 5.

is quiet and more than one ball (ideally 3) can be used on each hole (N.B., ssssh-hhh, don't tell the committee). Each game starts on the fairway, rather than on the tee and therefore par for each hole is 3. The game has five levels of increasing difficulty (see below), and the goal was to try and complete all five levels in as few holes as possible. Level 1 (Hole 1) requires three numbered balls to be dropped in three places: the centre of the fairway, one yard in the right rough, and one yard in the left rough 150 yards from the pin. Each ball is hit in turn onto the green (hopefully!) and then when reaching the green, played in turn to a finish (i.e., sink each ball before moving onto the next one). The combined score is then taken, with 3 pars, meaning that the level has been achieved and the player moves up to Level 2 (160 yards) on Hole 2. However, a 1 under par score means to move up two levels; 2 under par, go up three levels, whilst birdies with all three balls would be rewarded by going up four levels. Similarly, any bogey scores would result in the player moving back down levels, commensurate with the number of shots over par. The game is over when the player achieves a score of 9 on Level 5.

When watching Paul play this game, it was interesting to see how engaged he was, and how his emotions and intentions were influenced by the relative importance of each shot. For example, on the 1st Hole, Paul hit the ball from the centre of the fairway to five feet, giving himself one definite birdie opportunity, but he only managed to make the front of the green with the ball from the right rough, leaving a tough breaking putt from 25 feet. However, with the third ball, from the left rough, he missed the green long and finished in a 'valley' below the green and left himself a very challenging up and down. Remember, Paul can choose to take the balls in whatever turn he decides and he decided to start with the ball closest to the hole, knocking it in for birdie. This left Paul with two pars to make in order to move up a level. He was now faced with an interesting decision, take the easier ball that was on the green or hit the most difficult ball at the back of the green first and try and make his up and down, leaving the relatively easy ball to last. Paul decides to continue his strategy of taking the easiest ball first, however, he misjudges his putt leaving himself a very tricky 8-footer. Despite being annoyed with himself for making this so hard, Paul calms himself and picks the right line and pace and confidently rams the ball into the back of the cup. Now for the hard bit. The tariff for the shot is very high requiring a delicate flop shot that is going to have to land within a foot of the edge of the green to enable it to run down to the hole; land it any further and it will run down to the front of the green and make par almost impossible. Paul scopes out the shot and goes through his pre-shot routine, rehearsing the shot and using his imagery skills to feel and see the ball flight and roll he wants. Stepping up to the shot, it is noticeable how deeply he is focussing and is completely oblivious to my attempts to distract him by reminding him how hard this shot is. I note that his level of concentration is almost childlike. He steps up to the shot and nails it (almost) perfectly, landing the ball just on the green but not getting the exact length of roll he was hoping for. He now needs to sink a 6-footer to make the level – another clutch shot. He steps up and although he does not hit it as confidently as the previous putt, the ball safely drops in the hole. Paul smiles, and explains "wow" that was some challenge! He moves on to the next hole and the more difficult 160-yard Level. Reflecting on the game afterwards, we agree that it achieved exactly what we wanted from it, asking him to make challenging mid-to-long irons into the green, but because each shot had consequences, as he then had to finish off the hole he was completely engaged in, he then had to deal with significant emotions and make some tough decisions which closely simulated the experience of Tournament play.

Goal 5: Starting Fast: The Six-Hole Challenge

The Pro Analysis of the PGA tour 2018 (Hunt, 2018) reveals that the first six holes of a tournament and the first six holes on the subsequent days are highly correlated with success in the competition. From a psychological point of view, early success can strongly influence confidence and will influence how a golfer approaches the rest of the round. According to the data, tournament winners start fast and typically play more aggressive golf, but what does this mean? Starting fast indicates that the winning golfer gets into minus figures early in the round and, by implication, does this by playing more aggressively. A key challenge when trying to interpret this approach is what do we mean by 'aggressive'? A brief poll of some of our coaching mates shed little light on the concept, with 'risky', 'going for it', 'committed', 'high risk', 'low percentage shots', and 'going for the green on short par 4s' all being used as a substitute; synonyms of aggressive include assertive, forceful, energetic, dynamic, or competitive. Consequently, given this wide range of opinions, aggressive golf can mean different things to different players, however, we suggest that what aggressive play is for one golfer might be conservative for another and will be strongly influenced by the context of a player's psychological state and his/her skill set in interaction with the situation. Hitting a driver down a narrow fairway may seem like a very aggressive shot for one golfer and completely safe to another. To clarify our position, we like the www.dictionary.com definition:

Aggressive means; making an all-out effort to win or succeed; competitive.

We think this definition captures the mindset needed when a golfer sets out to win rather than avoiding losing. Or put another way, an aggressive golfer looks to compete, and this means giving themselves the best chance of making a good score. Consequently, we want the golfer to develop a positive mindset where they are always looking to find ways to win rather than avoid losing. Where they are looking to make birdies rather than avoiding making bogeys. Bogeys are obviously a significant detriment to scoring low, and of course, there are times when aggressive golf shaped around competing means accepting par or even bogey; however, overall, we would argue that designing games to explore their performance boundaries will help the player find the sweet spot in terms of the correct level of aggression for them.

So, going back to our initial discussion about the importance of starting fast and aggressively, we would remind the reader that being more aggressive does not mean playing high-risk golf, but it does suggest that easing into a tournament/round by playing conservatively may not be the best strategy on tour if the goal is to win or even qualify for the cut. With livelihoods on the line, the importance of making birdies is highlighted by looking at the winning scores and the score needed to simply make the cut. Indeed, if we look at the stats on all four of the main men's tours in 2018 (PGA, web.com, European Tour & Challenge Tour) the average winning score was -17 $+/-1$ and the average cut was just under level par $+/-4$. Therefore, for a professional golfer to make money on any of these tours they must be under par for the first two rounds (golf course and environmental conditions dependent of course).

One caveat here, is that the golfer needs to do their homework when working out a plan in advance of a tournament. Essential to this process would be looking back at scores in the tournament over the last few years as well talking to players, coaches, officials or commentators who were involved, to create a more complete understanding of the demands of the course. For example, last year's scores might have been high due to the set-up of the course being adjusted to make it more difficult due to the excessively low scores of the year before, so scores may not be reflective of how the course is 'playing' this year. Hence, all the information needs to be sifted, including knowledge gained from practice rounds to inform the initial beliefs about what it is going to take to qualify/win and hence underpin the planning of an appropriate strategy for each golfer.

Tour Data

The importance of adopting a positive approach to scoring for the professional player can be revealed by considering the scores in the PGA Tour feeder tour, the web.com tour, we introduced earlier in the chapter. Arguably, this is one of the most difficult tours to 'get out of' as only the top 25 money earners are automatically awarded a card for the PGA Tour. Hence, the pressure to make the cut and appear as high on the leader board as possible can be enormous, especially as prize money is top-heavy and the expenses to play on the web.com or the Challenge Tour are considerably high. Crucially then, *every shot counts*. For example, in 2018, 34 players on the web.com tour averaged under 70 per round, with a further 71 players under 72. Given that on this tour, the field in the final two days is reduced to the top 65 players (and ties), an analysis of the 2018 scores shows that to simply qualify for the final two days of tournaments requires, on average, an under-par score (-0.45) with a range of -5 to $+3$. To actually win the tournament you need to make an average score -16.7 with a range of -7 to -26. Clearly, golf at the highest levels requires significant levels of skill as well as the mental skills to thrive in such a demanding, pressure-filled environment.

A Birdie Fest

Given the standard of play needed to compete on the main men's tours, under par golf is not a bonus, but a necessity for survival. To put this into perspective, in 2019 on the web.com (at the time of writing), 142 listed players had completed 3,712 rounds with a total of 14,232 birdies – an average of 3.83 birdies per round. The top player (Xinjun Zhang) had 175 birdies in 38 rounds, whilst the joint 10th best players (Bo Hoag and Vincent Whaley) had 151 from 38 and 138 from 34 rounds, respectively (3.97 & 4.05). The three players ranked joint 65th for birdies and made the cut-number were Martin Flores and Billy Kennerly with 102 from 26, and Chad Ramey with 102 from 30. Just to make the cut you need to score 3.4–3.92 birdies per round.

The Game

When the competition and quality of play are so fierce, any golfer who aims to compete and stay on the tour must be ready to perform his/her very best from the first tee. As we highlight in the introduction to this section, it has been suggested, via scoring analysis of winners on the PGA Tour, that a good start, specifically the first 6 holes, is an important attribute for winning on a tour. To address these aims and in an attempt to (1) invite players to adopt a positive mindset where they looked to play with the right level of aggression aggressive golf (remember this related to our definition), and (2) to learn how to play with the emotions produced with this style of golf, we developed the Game of Sixes. As the name suggests, this game lasts six holes with the winner being the player with the lowest score at the end of the game. Table 4.4 (below) summarises a scenario which was recently played out by two potential tour players who were +4 golfers. Ensuring there are consequences to the result is a key part of this game. For example, playing for 'prizes' that are paid for from an 'entry fee' is a common method we use, however, there are many other ways we create 'consequences' that are relevant to the individual or group, one for another book! Variations to the rules can also be made to the games. For example, point rewards can be offered for birdies or eagles and the importance of birdies early in the game can be emphasised by providing decreasing rewards from Hole 1–6. For example, a birdie on Hole 1 could attract a one-point addition, Hole 2; 0.6, Hole 3; 0.6, Hole 4; 0.4, Hole 5; 0.2, and Hole 6, a zero-point addition. Manipulating task constraints in this way can shape the method in which each golfer attempts to solve the game problem.

In the example, Player B took an early lead with a 19-foot birdie on the 1st whilst Player A missed his. Both players par the 2nd, before A hits his tee shot to 3 feet on the 3rd hole and levels the match with an easy birdie. Player A moves into the lead as a reward for taking on the water in front of the green on the par 5 in 2, whilst player A, laid up and two-putted for par. However, player A immediately gives the shot back on the 5th after missing the green from 175 yards and

TABLE 4.4 An exemplar of scoring in the Game of Sixes

Hole	Par	Distance (yards)	Player A		Player B	
			Score	Overall score	Score	Overall score
1	4	405	4	Level	3	−1
2	4	380	4	Level	4	−1
3	3	180	2	−1	3	−1
4	5	500	4	−2	5	−1
5	4	320	5	−1	4	−1
6	4	450	3	−2	5	Level
Final score			22	−2	23	−1

finding the heavy rough. Player B continues with his low-risk strategy and makes par to stay −1. One important rule now comes into play in that if the scores are tied after 6 holes, the player who started the fastest is rewarded and the result is determined by countback, that is, the winner is the player who took the lead first. Consequently, as player B was in the lead after the first hole, he would win the match by matching player A's score, whereas Player A needs to win the hole.

In our example, the 6th hole is a 450-yard par 4 into a headwind which requires an accurate shot to a narrow fairway off the tee. Fairway bunkers are in play on the right side of the fairway. It is a demanding tee shot even for the best of players and, consequently, emotions and intentions of the golfer come into play and can impact the performance. The task demands impact differently on our two golfers. As he is behind and has nothing to lose, Player A plays with complete freedom and no fear, taking a driver with the goal of ripping it as far as possible. His bravery is rewarded and he finishes up in the light rough with a monster drive of 320 yards. In contrast, as he only needs to draw the hole to win, B decides to 'play safe' and takes his 3 wood. However, his defensiveness manifests itself in a 'tight' swing which reduces his club head speed and although he finishes on the fairway he only hits the ball 250 yards, leaving a shot of 200 yards into the green. Hitting first, B now has a change of mindset and realises he has to hit a top-notch approach shot to put pressure on A, who he believes now has a realistic birdie opportunity. He hits a confident 5 iron and manages to hit the green but is still left with a 30-foot breaking putt. A, meanwhile take his pitching wedge and flies the ball at the pin, finishing inside 6 feet. On the green, B feels he must make the putt and goes hard, but misses left, running five feet past the hole, resulting in a bogey. A then sinks his 6-footer for birdie and the win by two shots.

Summarising the Results

The narrative is informed by the data revealed in the Pro analysis of the PGA Tour (see Table 4.2 earlier in the chapter) and the understanding that the interacting individual, environment, and task constraints uniquely impact the intentions, emotions, and actions of each golfer. In terms of the tour data, Player A is rewarded for a more 'aggressive' strategy from the tee box (hitting driver more often) and this supports the data that shows that players who hit driver more often record better scores. While this is counter to the 'play safe' lobby, as the data show there is a strong correlation with distance off the tee and birdies made at the same time, the evidence supports 'going for it' at the expense of playing safe, which often does not produce as well as would be expected. Data show that hitting driver is more rewarding than taking a 3-wood and laying up, which is often not as accurate as one would envisage. So, the benefits of hitting long is not rocket science, if a player hits his/her driver into a spot that leads to a shot to the green with a shorter iron or wedge, that is, an easier club to control and provide an opportunity to hit it closer to the hole and score better. This is seen in our game with Player A being rewarded for taking a driver, whilst, Player B is not as accurate as he would have hoped and hits shorter. Similarly, the correlation with driving distance and length of putt is illustrated here, with the longer drive of B, resulting in a shorter putt for birdie. Additionally, the impact of task constraints (being ahead or behind) on the intentions, emotions, and actions of each golfer throughout the game, but specifically in terms of the critical last hole, provide some interesting findings of how the player reacts in such 'high pressure' situations for the player and coach to work on Of course, with the exception of a holed putt, every shot requires a decision that will impact the next shot and players need to be highly attuned to the dynamic interacting constraints (Figure 4.6).

The Game of Sixes x Three

Of course, by utilising a standard round of golf, the players can play three sets of six, with the winner being the one who wins the most sets (1 point for the first two sets with 2 points for the last set, meaning the player who is 2-0 down after two games can still draw and force a play-off or win on count back of most birdies in the 18 holes). Playing a second and third set provides opportunities for the golfer to immediately 'put right' the lessons from the previous set, enhancing the learning experience.

Variations-The Tournament

Whilst the simplest form of the game is a 1 versus 1 match, the task lends itself well to provide competition for a squad or group of players. The game can be played by as many players as required who can play in pairs, threes, or as four balls. To increase the representativeness of the game, the coach could set up leader boards on Holes 1, 3, and 5, which will encourage players to take into account their current status when making decisions on the course.

Variations-Last Man Standing

In this variation, the first six holes have a direct impact on the following 12, much like real tournament stroke-play golf. In the case of the example provided below (see Table 4.5), the par is 72 with par being 24 for the first game (of 6 holes) and 48

FIGURE 4.6 Decisions, decisions. The status of the golfer in a competition in interaction with his/her action capabilities. Here, the decision for the golfer is should they try and go over the bunkers on the left and the water on the right or lay-up, leaving a longer shot into the green.

for the second game (the following 12 holes). To qualify to win, the player must not exceed a total of 72 strokes over the full 18 holes. However, the number of shots allowed in the second game is determined by the score in the first. What you score in the first 6 holes leaves the number of strokes you have to play with for the following 12 holes. For example, if the golfer is −3 or −4 after game 1, they will have 48 shots to play with, whereas if they shoot +2 or worse they will only have 38 shots to play with. Once the players go 'bust' his/her score goes over 72, he or she is out of the competition and stops playing. This game was tailored for a group of Challenge Tour players and was based on training them for winning on the tour (−4 per round or better). You can adapt this game to your ability level or even use your handicap.

If playing in a group tournament, then the winner is the player furthest round the course after everyone is eliminated. If more than one player

TABLE 4.5 The relationship between shots taken in the first 6-hole game and the final 12 holes. The better your score in the first game the more shots you have to play with in the second

First 6 holes score	Shots to play with for final 12 holes
−3 or −4	48
−1 or −2	45
+1 or level	43
+2 or worse	38

completes the 18 holes, the winner is decided on the shots left in hand. If scores are tied, then the winner is the one who was leading after game 1. If the scores are still tied the result is decided on the total number of eagles and birdies made by each player.

Adaptations of this game can be tailored to the difficulty level of the course and the ability level of the players and, as already mentioned, handicaps could also be tailored into this game. Many other adaptations can be made, for example, if you only have time for 9 holes, halve the parameters of the game. Ideally, the challenge of any game should be just on the edge of a player or a group of players' ability. Hypothetically, you could also play this game in 'your head' every time you play.

Closing the Loop-The Debrief

An important part of the coaching process is debriefing after each set or game. Coaches should encourage players to rate the effectiveness and reflect on what they did well and what could they do better next time. Coaches may invite players to consider how they used information from the environment to guide their intentions and actions. For example, how well they read the wind, how they took into consideration the scoreboard or if they had a feel for their own emotions and its impact on their swing; how well they had planned the round in terms of course management and which holes they were going to target for birdie opportunities (or even eagles). An important part of this reflection process is for each player to check how 'ready' he/she was physically and mentally on the first tee, and if they were not, what they need to do differently next time. A key to success in these high-pressure performance environments is the ability to play well when emotions are heightened, to be able to swing freely, when the game is on the line, and to sink the 4-footer for birdie or par. Players need to know what it is like to play with fear, nerves, anger, happiness, dejection, excitement, and fulfilment. Learning, therefore, underpins 'knowing' themselves in performance environments, knowing how their emotions change what they see and what they miss, knowing how they think during the ups and downs of competing and knowing how their body behaves under pressure. The Game of Sixes provides such learning opportunities and invaluable performance data on which to co-design sporting practice tasks with their players.

Summary of the Game

Given the high standard of play required to simply survive, never mind thrive on the pro tour, the mindset of a tour golfer, as seen in any elite performer, needs to be flexible and aware of his/her current capabilities as determined by the demands of each tournament. However, what is evident from scoring averages seen on all men's tours discussed previously, is that professional golfers need to maximise their birdie opportunities to flourish on tour. To achieve this goal, it is suggested that to win on the PGA Tour, a fast start in a round is more beneficial to the pro golfer's chances of success, not just from the psychological boost a strong start can bring them. The Game of Sixes was developed to provide a realistic simulation where the dynamic interaction of intentions, emotions, and actions prevalent in the competition are replicated in practice. Consequently, this practice game and the competitive environment it creates is specifically designed to maximise traits that are seen to be beneficial on tour increasing the likelihood of transfer from practice to performance.

Overall Summary and Key Points

It is three years since Paul began his programme and the journey and has expected it has not been without its ups and downs. As expected, initially Paul struggled on the Duke's golf course as it was a course length he was not used to playing. However, he understood the rationale for using this course to accelerate his development, so he soldiered on despite his confidence taking a hit at times. It was important for Paul to understand that this was normal when the principle of overtraining or stretching his practice was central to the process. So, we worked really hard on supporting him when his performance dipped and his expectations and perceptions about his own ability were threatened. Over time though, he did begin to adapt and we kept challenging him, regularly changing the cut line in scenario-based four-day 'tournaments', until eventually, he had to play to −5/−6 to make the cut and then score −15 to 'win'. Paul's improvement was also clear from a statistical perspective with performance data showing that his driving had improved (fewer penalty shots and tighter dispersion) with similar improvements in his mid/long iron accuracy. After three years of this training, Paul has slowly progressed on the Euro Pro tour, culminating in this year (2019) being his best season ever. He finished high enough in the Order of Merit, for him to play five tournaments in the grade above, the Challenge Tour, in 2020. We are all pretty excited with where Paul can eventually end up playing.

Key Points

- Tour courses are generally much longer than club courses.
- Creativity is needed to simulate the demands of longer courses.
- Practice needs to create the same challenges as those on the tour.
- Don't waste practice time, make every shot matter.
- Play with consequences.

5

WORKING WITH HIGH-PERFORMANCE GROUPS

Section 1 – Thoughts, Theory, and Rationale of Working with High-Performance Training Groups

Introduction

In this chapter, the focus will move on to how I (GM) work with high-performance training groups (HPTGs). These training groups typically include 'elite' amateur players, college golfers, and mini-tour professionals who have the commonly stated aim of transitioning to the next level of performance and playing golf for a living. As such, the thinking that I apply to underpin the design of training sessions for these groups is easily applicable to those who coach regional and national squads, who work with collegiate teams, or anyone who has an interest in creating HPTGs for ambitious players they may know or work with.

In the first part of this chapter, I will talk about my philosophy in relation to the mindset and approach I take when working with my HPTGs which is strongly influenced and aligned to the key principles of ecological dynamics and its role and place in the application of a non-linear pedagogy. The chapter goes on to look at the design principles I use to develop my sessions and the thinking and rationale behind my practices. In the final part of the chapter, I introduce some specific session plans and games that I use with elite performers. It is not the intention to present this chapter in such a way that the reader feels like they are being instructed to replicate these sessions. Instead, it is hoped that you will feel inspired to design your own session, based on your own interpretation of what makes a high-level performer using the CLA framework.

Philosophy of the Training Group Concept

Much of the thinking and inspiration for the work I do with my 'training groups' has come from drawing on the past through speaking with players who played the game at high level. These players formed communities that would get together in the off-season or off weeks. The purpose of such groups would emphasise providing the stimulus to engage in the sport for the long hours needed to get good at it, but more crucially, provide the participants with the essential competition needed to sharpen up their games so that they could play well when it mattered. The groups would be made up of players who were walking the same path, with the shared goal of progressing in the game and furthering their careers at a professional level. Padraig Harrington credited one such group he was part of as being crucial, specifically in terms of how he had developed such a good short game (Woolly, 2014). The practice conditions of his group were one in which, if you couldn't hole putts for money you had to leave his group – you couldn't afford to stay. This type of practice ticks all of the boxes for designing representative learning task and the associated intentions and emotions captured in Affective Learning Design (ALD) (Headrick et al., 2015). Figure 5.1 provides an example of how coaches and players can capture emotions in golf in learning situations.

Deliberately, my 'training groups' are low-tech in nature – there are no video cameras, launch monitors, or training aids. Players leave their mobile phones in a box in a hut; they are cut off from the world for the duration of the training. I don't measure anything or keep statistics (more on this later); the performance is only relevant to the day of the training and your ranking vis a vis the performance of the other players in the group and the levels set by the various games we play. The environment is as basic as possible, and suboptimal conditions are valued highly. That means I don't want perfect greens and playing conditions – I want the training environment to be worse than the conditions of the real game. Here I draw comparisons with Pele, the Brazilian footballer and one of the greatest players of all time, who described the high-quality playing surfaces at his first World Cup as making the game feel easy when compared to the tight, uneven surfaces he played on as a child. In golf terms then, why would we want players to practice on easy courses and greens that are better than those they may experience in a tournament? I want training to be harder and more challenging than the real game so that players learn to 'tough it out'. This idea emphasises the importance of challenging players and pushing them towards 'instability' and forces them to search for new solutions that link to the CLA Principle 4: Repetition without Repetition.

Within my sessions, plans change on a whim and players don't know fully what to expect on any given day. This is deliberate on my part so I can help players learn to deal with the random and unexpected events that will most likely happen to them on and off the course during their careers. Experienced members of the group know to pack sustenance as scheduled breaks are often cancelled. The group

Golf Learning & Emotions Questionnaire (GLEQ)

Instructions:

Below is a list of words that represent a range of feelings that might be experienced during learning to play golf. Please carefully read each word and indicate on the scale (0-4) how you feel *right now, at this moment in time in relation to the current task/session.* There are no right or wrong choices. All selections should be based on your feelings alone.

	Not at all	A little	Moderately	Quite a bit	Extremely
Happy	0	1	2	3	4
Nervous	0	1	2	3	4
Satisfied	0	1	2	3	4
Annoyed	0	1	2	3	4
Fun	0	1	2	3	4
Stressed	0	1	2	3	4
Fulfilled	0	1	2	3	4
Angry	0	1	2	3	4
Joyful	0	1	2	3	4
Pressure	0	1	2	3	4
Successful	0	1	2	3	4
Frustrated	0	1	2	3	4
Enjoyment	0	1	2	3	4
Fearful	0	1	2	3	4
Accomplishment	0	1	2	3	4
Excited	0	1	2	3	4
Achievement	0	1	2	3	4

SCORING INSTRUCTIONS (for coaches only)		Score
Enjoyment	= (Happy+Fun+Enjoyment_Excited)/5	____
Nervousness	= (Nervous+Stress+Pressure+Fear)/4	____
Fulfillment	= (Satisfied+Fulfilled+Successful+Accomplishment+Achievement)/5	____
Anger	= (Annoyed+ Angry+Frustrated)/3	____
	Total GLEQ Score	____

FIGURE 5.1 Checking emotions during learning and performance can be a useful tool to make sure that the coach is creating affective learning. The Golf Learning Emotion Questionnaire is adapted from Headrick et al. (2015) and is a tool that can be used to provide a quick check at key moments during a practice session or round. Results can be used by coaches and sport psychologists to inform their learning design.

needs to self-regulate; new players to the group are often quickly put in their place if they complain or if their focus and intensity fall below the level of the more established players. Physical and mental fatigue at the end of a training day is valued higher than the level of performance. When a player enters the environment of the training group, I want it to be as raw as possible. There is nowhere to hide in the group as you are always being judged on your performance, and, as much as possible, I want to normalise the feeling of being exposed and helping players get comfortable with feeling uncomfortable. There is no coach intervention during activities, so, if things aren't going well, I want to help develop players who can learn to self-repair and work out how to stabilise their performance in the absence of external input. Stabilisation can often come in the form of the realisation that a tactical change is needed or that they need to work with what they have on the day. As much as possible, I want the change to be induced by the interaction between the player and his task, the environment, the struggle with him/herself, and their interactions with others. Briefly linking back to theory, these examples highlight that the player-environment 'system' is dynamic and even small changes in specific constraints can create instability as constraints interact and lead to reorganisation of perception and action and intentions and emotions.

The Elephant in the Room: Technical Problems

Before I get to the stage of talking about the methods I utilise in my application of the CLA, I believe there is a need to deal with the elephant in the room, when working with elite-level golfers, when things aren't going to plan which is the issue of the coach focussing on making technical swing changes as being the way to solve performance problems, or as a way of elevating performance to a higher level. The debate relating to the role of 'technique' and as such the issue of making technical changes has raged on in the golf world for a long time. As such it is important that, as coaches, we are clear about and can articulate our thinking in this respect. The first question that perhaps inevitably I pose when a player tells me they need to make technical changes, is whether the player actually has any technical deficiencies that need to be ironed out in order to help them progress their game. It is my contention, largely speaking, that elite-level players have already solved the problem of how to hit the ball well and as such have a 'technique' that is good enough to enable them to progress in the game. For example, many young professionals new to an elite professional tour seem to default to making technical changes as soon as things don't go well, even though their swing was good enough to get them to the tour in the first place (see Figure 5.2). For example, former Scottish tour player, Callum MacAuley, was part of the team who in 2009 won the Amateur World Championships at Royal Adelaide in Australia, and then went through all three stages of the European Tour Qualifying School, playing 252 holes in total, to secure his card for the 2009 European Tour. Clearly, Callum could play! However, like many golfers new to the tour, he struggled, and in his own words fell into the trap of focusing on technique changes before realising he would be much better off trusting the game that got him on the tour. Unfortunately, Callum quit tour golf in 2017, and shortly before he quit, he reflected on where it had gone wrong:

> I had a sit-down with the best Scottish golfer of all time back when I was just breaking through. Colin Montgomerie told me not to change anything

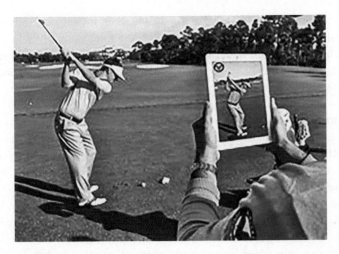

FIGURE 5.2   The over focus on technical correction at the expense of learning to be adaptable is a major problem for many struggling tour players. (In our opinion!).

about myself: not my swing, my coach, my preparation — nothing. Just trust what had made me successful. I listened to that for a while but, after a few months, I started making wee changes here and there and then, before I knew it, I was totally changing my swing, trying new clubs, changing my practice routine and it all just became a huge mess. That's where I went wrong.

(Crow, 2016)

From my many dealings with players who have struggled to make the transition to tour-level golf, I would say that Callum would not be on his own in seeing swing changes as a solution to tour woes and the struggles of adapting to tour life. Personally, I believe that Callum had everything he needed to be successful on tour and this is neatly captured him in his online blog in 2012 (MacAuley, 2020)) where he reflected on his performance at The Pacific Rubiales Columbia Championship. Here Callum had a good week tying 14th, especially given the challenging weather at the start of the week which meant tough conditions to score low. Here is what Callum had to say:

Colombia last week was an interesting adventure. With all the flights, buses, police escorts and 45 mph winds. I played far from my best golf, especially on Sunday, but once again I gave myself a chance going into the final round, and I have no doubt that if I keep doing that, my time will come. It was a very tough week, with a strong wind gusting off the sea all week, there was a high premium on cut off swings, solid putting and a hell of a lot of patience. I played decent on Friday and Saturday, stayed calm

> in testing conditions, but I learned a lot about myself on Sunday. I played really poor, and as bad as I've played in a long time, but I hung in and struggled through it and shot 2 over. Although it wasn't the final round I was looking for, I comfortably could've shot 85. I hung in, made a lot of saves and got out of my round what I could.

His performance in this event, more than anything, captured why I feel that Callum had all the attributes he already needed to play high level tour golf. He dealt with the multitude of disruptions associated with being a high-level golfer, such as long-haul flights, buses, police escorts, and 45 mph winds. He adapted his swing to deal with the strong gusting winds and he putted solidly (a must on tour) and in the face of all this, he remained patient. More importantly, he played worse than he had in a long time and turned what could have been an 85 into a 2 over par, 74, which gave him an excellent 14th place finish for the week. If ever there was a set of markers, or tick boxes that indicate the attributes you need to do well on tour, Callum potentially ticked them all in this event.

Experiences such as Callum's have led me to ensure that during my early exchanges when working with a new player who wants to join my HPTG, I impress upon them that all tour players have unique swing patterns and that if you started out with a clean slate you wouldn't set out to teach them the ones they have adopted. However, I strongly make the point that each one works for them, or they learn to work with it, and it isn't the swing that determines whether they win or lose. I emphasise my point by highlighting that many high-level sports have example after example of high performers with their own unique solutions to solving movement and performance problems. Once we have agreed that there is no such thing as the perfect swing, I impress upon them my belief that the fact they have reached the level that they have means they have already 'solved the problem' of how to hit the ball, but what they have yet to solve is the challenge of reaching or sustaining a high-performance career.

Building on the interactions highlighted above, I reinforce my belief to the players, they need don't need to "change what they've got, but they need to change what they do with what they've got." That is to say, they have reached a level of technical proficiency in the game to get to where they have, but perhaps, they now need to be better at the high-level decision-making and tactical sides of the game. Alternately, perhaps they need to develop better strategies to deal with the mental pressure they face on the golf course, rather than making elusive technical swing changes in the belief that it is some sort of magic bullet that will propel them to stardom. So, how do these ideas frame my coaching with the training groups? Below I present some of my ideas.

As a subscriber to a CLA as my frame of reference, when working with a golfer I would argue that it is the task that builds the action, and that there is no need to develop the action in isolation from the performance environment (see Chapter 1). Hence, specific golf shots emerge as a function of the individual constraints (size, power, confidence, perceptual skills) interacting with the task constraints (hitting a golf ball into a hole in as few strokes as possible), and environmental constraints (e.g. climate, weather, surfaces). Thus, technique emerges as a player searches for an effective coordination pattern to solve the performance problem to bring about a successful outcome. Therefore, technique development or rather skill acquisition should not be viewed as a 'thing' but instead as a 'process' of finding solutions to a wide range of performance problems.

Understanding the 'Game they Are In' – The A-Game Myth!

Closely related to the issues of making technical changes and the associated pitfalls is the question of how often top players play in a tournament with what they believe to be, or close to being, their A-game? Over the years I have asked many players and tour coaches this question and the typical response is between 0 and 3 tournaments per year. It is worth noting that some of the players are amongst the best players in the world! A good example of this is seen in the comments of Jordan Speith when he capped off a Player of the Year season in 2015 by winning the Tour Championship and FedEx Cup playoffs. He concluded:

> I didn't feel comfortable striking the ball, whatsoever, today or this week... It was amazing that I competed with the way I felt over the ball.
>
> *(Fine, 2015)*

I have, therefore, come to think about the so-called 'A game' as something of an imposter and not as the player's friend. If a player's A game was a true friend, it would turn up when they most needed it, and yet top players tell us it is often nowhere to be seen. An interesting question then is that if playing well in tournaments is more about learning to find a way of scoring well when the swing is off, why do so many players head to the range with the sole focus of developing an optimal swing? This point relates to the conversation on the search for consistency in Chapter 3, and to me this reflects the traditional view of golf expertise and practice (irrespective of the ability level of the golfer). As I discussed at the beginning of the chapter, this further highlights the point that we as coaches need to ask ourselves as to why we push our players towards an attempt to reproduce their A game. We engage the player in so-called remedial technical changes, often breaking the swing down to practising specific phases of the swing (i.e. the take away or the position at the top of the back swing), using launch monitor data and block practice (i.e., repeating the same task over and over), when perhaps, a far more effective approach would be to help shape intentions around keeping them away from their A game and challenging them to function with their B, C, or even D game on the day (see Figure 5.3).

In designing training interventions that neither promotes the search for optimal functioning nor values the concept of it, I am trying to exploit the true potential of the human movement system and help ensure that expert golfers can spontaneously adapt their motor patterns as information (internal e.g., injury, joint stiffness, emotions; external, e.g., weather, climate, playing surfaces) nudges them into and out of different coordinative states. Crucially, I want to

FIGURE 5.3 Getting up and down is a key part of scrambling when a player is not on his/her 'A' Game. In my HPTGs we spend a lot of time putting players under pressure to close out holes.

help golfers be able to do this on a moment to moment basis, promoting the flexibility to quickly calibrate or 'tweak' their 'techniques' (to maintain a level of scoring conducive to performing well). This ability to adapt is exemplified by Gary Player who in conversation with world-renowned golf coach Cameron McCormick (the long-time coach of Jordan Speith) stated that he had won 165 professional tournaments in his career and:

> ...every tournament I won was with a different swing and a different feel... my warm up was always about finding a swing for that day...I can most positively tell you this...you never own [your swing] you are just renting it...
>
> *(Player, 2020)*

Similarly, Sir Nick Faldo (2019), talks about the need to have a plan B, describing it as has having 'armour' that can be taken to the course and ensures that you are ready to play by finding shots that work on any particular day. The capacity to be adaptable fits perfectly with the ideas of the CLA, as explained in Chapter 1. High skill emerges from a tighter and tighter fit of the individual with the environment as they develop the movement patterns and abilities that exploit the features of the specific golf environment. If we contrast this view of skill learning to the traditional approach in golf where movement patterns are repetitively drilled in a closed environment such as a driving range, then we are getting closer to understanding why golfers sometimes struggle to transfer their range practice to the golf course (McDowall, 2020). Consequently, when designing CLA sessions much of my time is spent thinking about creating training scenarios that invite the elite players to come up with movement solutions to deal with the unusual and unpredictable situations that seem to occur in almost every round of golf. This approach stops players from going through the motions and keeps them away from stability (in the actions, emotions and thinking) and the false comfort associated with this type of practice which leads them to believe they have access to their A-game whenever they want it. Essentially, I am trying to help my golfers feel comfortable, being uncomfortable.

Section Conclusion

This section has attempted to build a picture of some of the issues and (what I believe to be) the misconceptions of reaching and sustaining a high-performance career in golf. This has included a discussion on the potential pitfalls of chasing technical changes. Closely associated to this is the perhaps erroneous belief that tour players are playing with their optimal swing on a regular basis. In the next section, I go on to build the argument for the training activities I use. The ideas are based on what I believe to be some of the key strategic issues associated with playing high-level golf and are predicated on the notion and (in opposition to mythical A-games and elusive technical changes) that in order to be successful at Golf you need to use 'what you have on the day' because in that moment that is all you have access to!

Section 2 – RLD for HPTGs

Introduction

In this section I am going to outline how I use the CLA Principles when designing sessions with my HPTG. Rule No1 that I have always used as my guiding principle, that I always use as my guiding principle, relates to the foundation CLA principle 3: RLD, which is a central theme running across all chapters of the book. Consequently, I always say to myself that 'if it doesn't look like and feel like the real thing then don't do it'. In a CLA, this concept is known as RLD. This sentiment almost certainly comes from my early reading of the CLA literature and represents the first light-bulb moment in the development of my thinking. As a result, I always ask players after a training session, where a new game, task manipulation, or a new player has been introduced, whether they recognise the demands of the activity in relation to something they have encountered during tournament play. If the answer is no, then we simply don't do it again.

This section will go on to explain why, for example, if you came to watch a HPTG session you might see on your arrival the manipulation of the environment and the performer with a player wearing a high-visibility (Hi-Vis) vest, the presence of a whiteboard, a klaxon, multiple red cones, a stopwatch, or even a session that is being filmed and streamed on Facebook Live. On an odd occasion you may also find on arrival that a pre-session activity has already begun in an adjacent sports hall or field where students are being deliberately fatigued ahead of the HPTG session. The aim then of this section is to demonstrate how these ideas are related to the CLA and to working with HPTGs and then to describe the games and the rationale for the rules that form the significant task constraints. I will try to exemplify the point that the practical application of a CLA, when working with HPTGs, involves deliberately manipulating the constraints (information) impinging on the performer for the purpose of (hopefully) shaping their behaviour. It is hoped that the thoughts, ideas, and rationales will help you create your own powerful, engaging, and emotional learning environments.

RLD

Environment, Performer, and Task Constraints

When I design sessions for the HPTG, careful consideration is given to the information that is present and flowing in the training environment (e.g. the mental, technical, tactical, physical aspects of performance). The extent to which the information replicates that of the performance context is the very notion of 'RLD'. I think about the training environment as being a room that the player walks into and that room is full of information that they must familiarise themselves with before they can perform well there. Ideally, I have carefully crafted the room so that it closely replicates the information and challenges inherent in the player/s performance environment.

Creating representative learning environments is not easy if you haven't walked the walk and experienced a higher level of performance yourself. For this very reason, I value the opinions of the players with whom I work and always work with my players to 'co-construct' the training sessions. As highlighted by Tiger Woods:

> ...from a feel standpoint...I think I know a lot more than they do [coaches], because they've never played down the stretch of a major championship. What do the hands feel...what does the body feel...will they [suggested changes] work on the back nine on a Sunday of a major?
>
> *(Vuchi, 2014)*

As I have previously mentioned, much of my early thinking in relation to training and preparation came from speaking with players who played the game to a high level. The aim of doing this was to fill the gaps in relation to what I didn't know about what it is like to be a Tour player, to be on the road for several weeks at a time, to play four consecutive days with each round taking up to, and sometimes beyond, five hours, often interspersed with unscheduled delays in play. Likewise, I have never experienced the accumulation of stress and fatigue that builds up over the week of a tournament, not to mention what it's like to play in different time zones and the challenges associated with being 'on the road' for several weeks at a time.

The information I have received has led me to deliberately manipulate the performers' energy levels with the likes of pre-training fatigue sessions (where players are deliberately fatigued ahead of training). This was born out of a conversation with a former winner on the European Tour who described the effect fatigue had on his swing and decision-making towards the end of a tournament – particularly when he had been on the road for several weeks at a time. He suggested that it took him a long time to become attuned to this and understand how it affected him. He felt that that if he had been able to practice in a way that replicated these demands he would have performed better in his early tour career. I have also spoken to ex-tour players who experienced the same issues and would, therefore, play 36-holes continuously with a weighted carry bag during the off-season. As such, I regularly have the HPTG come in at 7am, two hours ahead of a 9am start, and have them complete a high intensity cardio session at 70%–90% of their maximum heart rate for 90 minutes. I would stress that these cardio sessions are designed and run by a health and fitness professional and with the complete knowledge of our performers' current health status.

The Leader Board

Other examples of creating representative learning opportunities during HPTG sessions are features such as using a whiteboard, a klaxon, a stopwatch, and the infamous red cones. The whiteboard is in fact a 'live' Leader board and this first made an appearance after one member of the group, (let's call him Lenny), returned from a high level tournament and for the first time had seen his name near the top of a Leader board on the course. According to him:

> When I'm playing at a high level in events around the world with different set up of tournaments you often see a leader board on the course and to see where you are is a big thing...everyone knows it takes a lot of time to get to the top of a Leaderboard and many pros might not even experience this in a year. I played in a tournament in South Africa, we turned up on practice day one and there were electronic Leaderboards all over the course. By Thursday afternoon I was leading by three shots, [but at that point in time] not knowing that I couldn't handle the pressure of seeing that I was the leader.

A Leader board is a visual indication of where you are positioned in a tournament and all that is implied by that, be it that you are in position to win or perhaps you can see where the projected cut is going to fall. Adding in a Leader board to the practice environment, therefore, affords different learning opportunities to

FIGURE 5.4 The Leader board. Creating a Leader board is a key part of making practice as realistic as possible to create the thoughts and emotions representative of those found in competition.

different players and realising that the presence of a constraint that many would feel is insignificant can lead to 'non-proportional' consequences for players (as highlighted by Lenny). Importantly, the presence of the Leader board, prompts each golfer to interact with the affordances provided in a way best suited to their individual constraints. This realisation has been perhaps the biggest positive learning for me as a practitioner applying a CLA and highlights that you simply can't predict what a player will learn or how they will go about solving a performance problem. For example, when I added the Leader board into the HTPG training sessions, it enabled them to become accustomed to seeing their name 'out-there' for all to see. It has gone on to becoming a standard feature of our training environment and has proved to be a critical constraint that has afforded us the opportunity to talk about and explore the nature of 'scoring' from a strategic point of view (Figure 5.4).

Exploring this further, the Leader board has also afforded the HPTG the opportunity to understand how performance fluctuates and how good scores are constructed. Learning 'how to score' is the biggest and most central facet of playing high level golf. Players have come to learn that patience is critical to scoring. In the early days of training with this approach, many players reflected that had they just stayed patient when trailing behind the leader in a training event they would have got closer than they did from taking a more aggressive approach. The visible Leader board has sent a message to the player that when they acted in an aggressive (given the discussion in the last chapter perhaps we should say 'high risk') manner it had seldom paid off. Some valuable lessons have been learnt regarding the nature of scoring – particularly in relation to the decision-making process. What has become apparent is that it is not necessarily birdies that win the training games with the elite group; instead it is typically the avoidance of making 'high' scores and hanging in until your 'luck' changes. I have run these activities for over a decade now and if there is one phenomenon in the data that repeats itself time and time again it is that successful players (those who win or get close to winning games) consistently avoid penalty shots, 3 putts, and taking more than one attempt to hit the green with approaches – as such avoiding running up high scores. More importantly the number of birdies made by a player does not in itself significantly differentiate where a player finishes in the game. In 2019, Justin Thomas led the PGA tours' birdie average with 4.58 birdies per round, good players make birdies there's no doubt about that (the 100th ranked on the birdie averages in 2019 was Bubba Watson who made just under four per round) (https://www.pgatour.com/stats/stat.156.y2019.html). For me, whilst there is a need to make birdies, eventual success will only come from limiting the number of over par scores and putting themselves in a situation where pars are almost guaranteed. By making sure they hit the green, they will automatically create birdie opportunities which will eventually result in them making some putts (get lucky for arguments sake), and as such gravitate towards the top of the Leader board. The pioneering course management strategist, Scott Fawcett (personal communication, 2019), recalls a story about Tiger Woods who on being asked what made him the best player in the world replied:

> ...because I was the best lag putter...I could just hit it to 20ft to 30ft toward the middle of the green, not make many stupid bogeys, kill the par 5's, shoot a few under every day and basically always be in the hunt.

Scott goes onto say that Tiger had intuitively figured this out which would seem to be consistent with the notion that experts have superior tacit knowledge and practical intelligence than lesser performers. If you can strategize and execute your shots 'well enough', thus, avoiding destructive high scores and exploit your strengths such as being long off the tee that turns Par 5s into par 4s, then probability starts to work in your favour. It is likely for example that when you reach a certain level of performance you will convert at least some of your good approach shots into birdies. A good score can then turn into a great score due to a little bit of luck by, perhaps, holing a long putt for an eagle or holing out from a bunker, or a slightly miss hit that finishes close to the hole for a tap in. In Daniel Kahneman's (2011), bestselling book, *Thinking fast and slow*, spikes in performance, such as going from a good score to a great score are associated with the statistical phenomena known as 'regression to the mean' and the role that random variance or chance plays in scores that are better than the statistical norm. The key point here is that luck/probability makes no difference to you, nor does a round containing 2, 3, or 4 birdies, if you've already made a raft of bogies or worse. The CLA in creating representative learning conditions has afforded the HPTG to learn this valuable lesson.

In summary, it is worth noting that the introduction of the Leader board was never meant to be the stimulus for much of the learning that I see taking place in our sessions, but that is the power of good representative training design as it throws up 'more' than you can foresee and can lead to consequences that are non-proportional in nature.

Perturbing Players

As I have described at the beginning of the chapter, top players have high levels of expertise and when playing with their A games seem to make the game look very easy. However, for me, the real champions are the ones who can find a way of scoring well when they encounter events or situations which have the potential to perturb or unsettle them. A perturbation is defined as *'a disturbance of motion, course, arrangement, or state of equilibrium.'* (*https://www.merriam-webster.com/dictionary/perturbation*) and in golf could relate to a change within the individual (mental or physical state), something that changes in the environment (wind, slow play), or a specific task constraint (a piece of bad luck like landing in a divot or a ball plugging in a bunker). Often, changes in internal states are impacted by the task or environment, however, sometimes players have to play with injury or 'niggles' that can act as distractions or mean that their 'signature' golf swing is not available and they need to find another way. A great example, was Tiger Woods who found a way to win the 2008 US Open with a broken leg and cruciate ligament damage. In round three Woods was paired with the Swede Robert Karlsson. His caddie Gareth Lord got a close-up view which he described in comments to *The Guardian* (Murray, 2018):

> Within the first four holes you knew because if he tried to hit a normal shot, he just couldn't do it," Lord recalls. "The only thing he had off the tee was a genuine 30-yard cut. That didn't seem to hurt him. The iron shots he could get away with a wee bit more but off the tee, he was in trouble unless he hit that big cut.
>
> The amount of people inside the ropes, especially over the last few holes, was incredible. It was like a Ryder Cup. He was literally playing on one leg, what he was doing out there was freaky and people were desperate to see it. He would chip in, hole a 60 ft putt...
>
> I remember the par-five 13th where he had hit it into a Portaloo off the tee, somehow [he] hit the green from 70 yards wide of where we were, then holed from 65 ft with 10–15ft of break. His putter was in the air with 20 ft to go. I walked off the green and there were blokes crying in the crowd.
>
> On the 18th tee he set up to the ball, he was about to go, said 'No' and began wiggling his knee like an Elvis impersonator. You heard this 'crack' ... Robert and I looked at each other. He then hit this sliding fade into the middle of the fairway. They both hit a five-wood to the back of the green.

Robert misses, Tiger holes it for an eagle. On the 17th he had chipped in from a bunker he could barely get out of, Steve Williams had to help him.

Remarkably, Woods would go onto win the event during an 18-hole playoff with Rocco Mediate and then was then out of the game for nearly eight months as he underwent treatment on a broken leg and torn anterior cruciate ligament. A broken leg is an extreme example of a perturbation acting to disturb the individual's ability to perform well. Whilst factors that have the potential to perturb players are obviously individual, there are several common themes that seem to disturb a player's equilibrium including slow play, wet weather, or gusting wind. For me, as a coach of elite players, it is therefore essential that I provide practice opportunities to prepare my players so they know they can handle such situations and how this shapes our thinking in terms of making practice as 'real' as possible. Hence, in my opinion, a good practice task/environment needs to afford the player the opportunity to practice and learn how to stabilise their performance when there are internal and external factors acting to disrupt them. To this extent the more ways you disrupt the performer, the more opportunities you afford them to act with creativity to bring about a stable level of performance (e.g. Tiger Woods playing a 30-yard cut with a broken leg).

In some respect, I believe that the progress a player is making towards becoming a successful tour player can be judged based on how easy it is to perturb them. The more difficult it is to do this, the more adaptive they become and demonstrate their capability to find solutions to performance problems that can't always be predicted in advance. Over the years, I have used several methods to perturb the players during training activities to afford them this learning opportunity. This philosophy was clearly articulated by a past member of the HPTG who responded to a question from another coach about what HPTG training was like. She responded with "Graeme spent most of his time trying to make me 'as uncomfortable as possible'". There are many ways in which this can be done and many of the ideas I have implemented have come from players reporting back about conditions that they have struggled with during tournament play. To understand what the training looks and feels like for the players, imagine going into a five-hour training activity, potentially after being deliberately fatigued, and being told to swap your golf equipment with your partner to simulate clubs getting lost or delayed in transit. You may find yourself playing with a set of clubs completely ill-designed to the dynamics of your body and your swing. My focus as a coach is therefore to see if a player can quickly adapt to this unforeseen perturbation or does it critically affect them and they are unable to perform? It is interesting to observe the different response that players have to this 'disruption' – on one occasion swapping clubs was too much for an 'ex' member of the HPTG and he got in his car and left the course in a huff – clearly being asked to deal with the challenges of high performance is not for everyone!

There are many other ways I have gone about disturbing the players' equilibrium in a way that is recognisable to the demands they will face in high level tournament golf. For example, I carry a stopwatch with me, and will randomly put a group on the clock if I feel they are playing too slow. It is interesting to observe the changes in behaviour particularly if the player/s are near the top of the Leader board. Another example of this is when I routinely enforce delays in training by setting off a klaxon. Often, I do this at critical points in time during the task, such as early in the session or before the players have had an opportunity to get any momentum going. Sometimes I do it late on when things are getting tense as the task nears its conclusion. The klaxon 'constraint' came about after many of the players reported there seemed to be more delays in professional golf versus amateur golf. Whether it be delays or suspension in play due to weather conditions, slow playing partners, or courses with bottlenecks in them, the main concern for many of the players was the ability, or inability, to 'switch back on' in these circumstances. Often a delay would be followed by a period of poor play which was extremely costly at that level. I introduced the klaxon to deliberately perturb the players by impacting their concentration and providing the condition that led to them switching off – affording them with the opportunity to learn how to 'switch back on'.

Manipulating Task Constraints

The final piece of RLD that I want to talk about is the manipulation of information in the environment through the use of task constraints and this is where I have become infamous with the HPTGs – my use of my dreaded 'red cones' (see Figure 5.5). Given my goal of pushing players out of their comfort zones, I use red cones as extra boundaries and hazards designed into the field of play. Specifically, I use the cones to play on the weaknesses of each golfer and make them pay more attention to their on-course decision-making and controlling the flight of the golf ball. Here I provide some examples of how I employ the second CLA Principle: Constrain to afford to show how I design-in constraints to manipulate the affordance landscape.

FIGURE 5.5 The red cones act as boundaries to emphasise the importance of decision-making and controlling ball flight.

For example, if a player has a tendency to get 'sloppy' when hitting into a green by not identifying the best landing areas, I will 'cone-off' areas and designate them as 'out-of-bounds'. Creating out-of-bounds or hazards puts the ability to control the ball into the context of making good decisions because of the potential to incur penalty shots. Many valuable lessons have emerged out of these types of affordances both for the player and the coach. As previously mentioned, players who do well in these tasks limit (or eradicate) penalty shots and learn to adapt to these to some extent in order to survive, and flourish in the HPTG – this attribute is non-negotiable. The design and manipulation of the task constraints is done so as to induce an adaption in key mechanisms (e.g. decision-making, control of emotions, concentration, patience, resilience) that control performance.

The manipulation of 'information' in the environment is also something I use during on-course training. Figure 5.6 illustrates this and the way in which RLD can be individualised to afford different players learning opportunities relative to their own weaknesses. In this example the players are playing the *close-out game* (see the close out game in the *HPTG Games* section); player A struggles with a snap hook left when under pressure and player B is struggling with distance off the tee under competition conditions. If Player A hits it out of bounds normal rules apply, whilst if Player B does not reach their distance target from the tee they receive a 1-shot penalty. Whilst they are both playing in the same activity, they must satisfy the demands of individualised constraints in order to bring about a successful outcome.

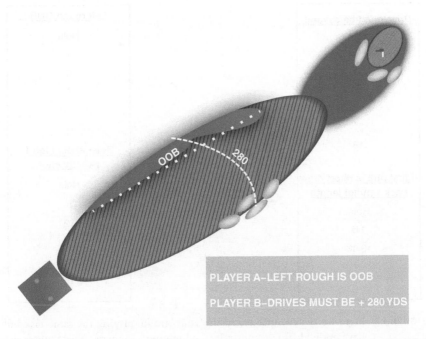

PLAYER A–LEFT ROUGH IS OOB

PLAYER B–DRIVES MUST BE + 280 YDS

FIGURE 5.6 The white dots represent 'red cones' and designate that the area to the left is out of bounds for Player A, and the cones at 280 represent the minimum distance Player B must hit off the tee to avoid being awarded a penalty stroke.

In this type of design, the smaller challenges of working with or addressing individual weaknesses are couched within the bigger challenge of completing the task. The number of holes you impose on these constraints is up to the coach and the player. I have found that the player must have some autonomy with regards to the difficulty and nature of the task (see Renshaw et al., 2012 for an in-depth discussion of how a CLA can meet the basic psychological needs of learners). The importance of co-constructing the rules is important as a player is unlikely to have the motivation to apply themselves and see the activity through if they perceive it to be too difficult and unachievable.

When designing the games, different holes may have different task constraints because you may want to work on more than one weakness at a time. For example, Player A may be struggling with a snap hook off the tee, but he may also be struggling with distance control for 70–100 yards and you may want to add in an extra constraint to challenge that particular issue. With this type of RLD, each player needs an individualised set of notes that gives them relevant information for the hole they are about to play (see Figure 5.7).

We will now go on to look at some of the tasks that I found work well with the HPTG over the years. The ideas above are designed to be used alongside a game and it is up to you what environmental task or performer constraints you add to any given game to meet the needs of your players.

Drive must be bevond 280	Left rough OOB
Hole	Hole
2	1
5	5
10	9
11	13
18	16
	Beyond pin high 1 penalty shot
If first putt is short draw back 1 putter length	Hole
Hole	5
1-6	12
13-18	14
	15
	18

FIGURE 5.7 Here we see two players in the same group, playing the same task but have individualised constraints impinging on them. These notes are printed and handed to each player on the first tee.

HPTG Games

A key factor underpinning my game design principles is the concept of *end-directed striving* or *intentionality;* a key principle in CLA session design (see Chapter 1). This concept simply means that we act with the end in mind, and we do so to try to bring about a successful conclusion to the set task. Why start here you might ask? Well, this concept, more than any other, has contributed to the success of the sessions I have undertaken with the HPTG. It is the single biggest reason, I believe, that my players report that they experience physiological and psychological overlap between the emotions they experience during training and those that they experience during performance. Hence, creating consequences that align with those found in competition settings are extremely important to design-in when attempting to create practice that is representative of competing.

Replicating the conditions of tournament golf is the element of session design that I am asked about most often. Coaches often tell me that they struggle to design sessions that have anything like the intensity or meaning of tournament golf. When the conditions of training replicate the demands of competition, they are emotion-laden (hot cognition) when compared to the emotionless (cold cognition) conditions of the golf driving range. Given that we see the world and move differently when we are emotionally engaged, developing awareness of how one will react in high pressure emotionally laden situations is crucial to becoming a good player (Headrick et al., 2015). Consequently, by creating practice environments that create the same intentions as this means that they experience the range of emotions just as they would in a tournament and learn to experience what playing is like under those conditions.

Let's look a little more closely at the powerful concept of *intentionality* and how I use it. First, it is possible to view in all human behaviour the *intentionality* of goal-directed behaviour – and sport is no different. There is likely no example of any human behaviour that doesn't begin with the end in mind. In the game of golf, as in all other sports, performers are converging on an end point (the cut or the end of the tournament), at which time judgements are made on that performance. Of course, as the end point gets closer, it brings with it the commensurate emotions and pressure.

As discussed in the last chapter, in a professional golf tournament, at the highest level, the player's first critical point of assessment is the 36-hole cut, at which point two-thirds of the field does not meet the required performance criteria to allow them to play in the last 36 holes. Failure to make the cut has significant financial implications as prize money is only awarded to qualifiers, but of course, the golfer still must pay the not inconsiderable costs associated with getting to and from and accommodation during the tournament. In conjunction with this, a larger sub plot is playing out in the background; failing to make the cut, negatively impacts their ranking on the Tour which could ultimately lead to a player losing their Tour privileges to play. In this respect converging on making the 36-hole cut is nested in the bigger goal of converging on retaining a Tour card (see Figure 5.8).

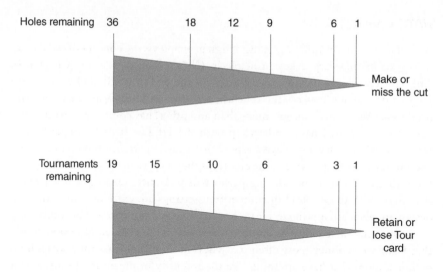

FIGURE 5.8 Illustration of working with intentionality towards an end goal, a well-designed practice task has this feature, and towards the narrow end of the cone the pressure builds, and everything starts to change.

This story of convergence and nested convergences is the context and conditions within which high level sport is played and runs through all levels of the game.

As such, I believe good practice must be based on *intentionality* and this will lead to observation of actions, emotions, and cognitions that are normally reserved for tournament play. Observing players in settings where the intentions are in line with tournament conditions affords the coach the opportunity to really get to know how players react under pressure and then work with the players during or post training to check and overcome any behaviours that may be limiting their potential and holding them back. A good example of how framing practice around intentionality was seen on one occasion during the close-out game (see below), where a very high-level performer had the opportunity to win the task on the 12th hole. Avoiding a bogey or worse on the Par 3, 12th would mean that he had the first opportunity to win the activity. He knew this, so did his playing partners and the group who were just putting-out on the 11th hole (I made sure of this). With the expectant crowd gathering around the green, he preceded to hit a 6 iron so far off the line to the right of the green that ball rolled down the embankment and into a position from which he didn't get up and down for a Par. This situation replicated the emotions of knowing that a Par could win you a tournament or when you need a Par at the last to make the cut. The player by his own admission, admitted that the pressure had got to him and he rushed his pre-shot routine to get the shot over and done with. This situation allowed us to connect the emotions he felt in that moment to a strategy for the next time he experienced them. We quite simply developed a strategy of feeling like he was doing things in slow motion in these situations whilst methodically sticking to his pre-shot routine.

Piecing this together now I will go onto talk about some specific tasks that I have designed that create representative learning experiences for the members of the HPTG. These ideas are merely a snapshot of what I do, and it should be remembered that what works with my groups, that is, level of intensity and difficulty, may not work with your players and as such task design always needs to be carefully thought out to match the ability of the group you are working with.

The Close-Out-Game

Essential to success on tour is the ability to close a round out when you know what you need to do. It is clear from talking to former players and our current group that during a tournament everyone knows 'the number' that is needed. This may be the number needed to make the cut, finish in a high spot in a tournament, or in fact to win a tournament. This game assumes the player 'has reached that number' and they 'know it'. So, the question the game is asking is can you, whilst in the knowledge of being 'on the number', close the deal out and finish on that number or better? The game was inspired by a conversation with a veteran of the European Tour who had retained his card for 14 years in a row. He talked about a common situation where when he was on 'the number' he would just 'coast it' in from there. Meaning, he would do nothing special for the remainder of the round and just see it out.

The goal of the game is to make 6 consecutive pars (or better), at which point the game is finished and the player can leave the course. However, the last par must be an up and down from off the green. This means that after a run of 5 pars or better the player can *close-the-game-out*, but they must do so by deliberately missing the green in regulation and then getting up and down to finish the task. Of course, the game can be played in many ways and doesn't need to be played over six holes. A key constraint on the progress in this game is that if the player takes a bogey or worse on any hole the game resets to zero. For example, if a player pars the first four holes but bogeys the fifth hole, the game resets and they start from zero on the sixth. This game is in fact more difficult than the real game because in real play a bogey could be followed by a birdie and the net situation would be level par. However, playing the game in this manner keeps the players on knife-edge and trains them beyond the needs of the activity. It is intended to put the players in stressful situations and places a demand on strategic thinking and their ability to 'coast it' out when they need to. One former member of the HPTG reflected that training in this manner had helped because

> …these tasks put me in even more stressful environments than when I compete, so competitions became easier and I've started to perform better.

Another variation on this game which I find works well and gets to the heart of learning how to score is when the game can only be closed out with a birdie. Elite-level players will find it relatively easy to make 5 pars in row on non-tour courses. In this variation once, and only once they have 5 pars or better, can they close the game out with a birdie. However, the birdie doesn't need to be straight after the run of five holes. If the player continues to make no worse than par, then the next birdie will close the game out. This means the player knows that a birdie is needed to finish the task, however, a bogey or worse would put them back to zero. This has led to some interesting conversations about the nature of scoring. The player is poised between attack and defence in this game. Not wanting to make a bogey but wanting to be close enough to have a chance at the birdie; or just hanging in their because they know a Par 5 is coming presenting a sure-fire opportunity to close the game out. Our conversations post-round are centred on the balance between positive and negative outcomes. Questions such as, what was your thinking today? What caused that fatal bogey that dropped you back to zero? Tell me about the birdie you made to complete the task? What would you do differently if you were in that situation again? Do you feel what you have learnt is transferable to the golf course? Providing opportunities to help players learn to deal with the psychological consequences of being in the lead is a novel approach to practice, but one I feel is extremely valuable. In essence, for the players I am working with who may be relatively new to tour golf experiencing being 'in the lead' may not happen too often, and I feel it is my role as coach to ensure that I have at least attempted to prepare them for what this feels like.

A fun way to play this game is to turn it into a competition by making the winner the player who takes the least number of holes to close the game out (six being the lowest possible). Imagine a situation where three out of eight players have passed through the 5-hole mark without taking a bogey or worse. When this happens, word always gets around to the other players in the other groups and the business of attack and defend becomes a more stressful and demanding situation. There are too many permutations that can emerge from this activity to discuss them all here and some of them can fall a little short of the level of 'representativeness' I like to achieve in my sessions; however, this has afforded us the opportunity to discuss some important issues such as where our focus should be during tournaments. Should it be on concerning ourselves with what others are doing? Should we be in our own bubble? Should we change our strategy and take on more difficult shots than we would normally? What is the success rate when we do this? One thing is for sure, there is no single answer to these questions. The key thing is the activity has afforded us the opportunity to discuss these issues with the players in such a way that perhaps isn't always possible with more traditional methods of training.

The Division 1 and 2 Game (D1 and D2) (Switch-on-Quick)

This is an activity that I do in our short game area. The game emerged out of conversations with members of the HPTG who were taking their first steps into professional golf. They noted that the greater strength and depth in professional golf meant that they couldn't just ease into a tournament and take 9 or 12 holes to effectively get warmed up (see The Game of Sixes in Chapter 4). It often didn't matter all that much being 3 or 4 over par after the first 9 in an amateur event, but that wasn't the case in the professional game. Being this much over par at the turn in a professional event probably means that it is highly likely that you will to need to play the next 27 holes considerably under par just to make the 36-hole cut. Giving away so many shots so early in a tournament brings about additional unwanted pressure, particularly, when you are playing for your living. At the very worst, being level par at the turn sets the rest of the round up in such a way that a couple of birdies during the back 9 can make for a good day of work. Therefore, on Tour, it pays to stabilise your performance quickly if for no other reason than that you are competing against a better standard of player.

In the worst-case scenario, you have gone to considerable expense to play a tournament in foreign country and after the nine holes of play you may effectively have missed the cut. If this pattern repeats itself week on week, not only does it cost a player considerable expense, but leads to an erosion of confidence that can be even more debilitating. Many top-level amateurs have turned professional and not been able to achieve the levels expected of them on Tour. The loss of confidence from missed cuts and subsequent financial pressure can end a career before it has begun. As a former top-level amateur told me:

> I turned professional off +5 and had achieved everything I could in the amateur game, I was full of confidence, I turned professional and missed my first few cuts and my confidence just went, I never really got it back.

The D1 and D2 game puts an emphasis on stabilising performance quickly. The consequence of not doing so will quickly result in a player getting relegated to the dreaded D2. The setup of this game depends on the facility you have available to you. I set up 2×4-hole courses (see Figure 5.9), each course has a range of shots from inside 100 yards to the green, and I change the range of shots every 15–20 minutes to prevent players becoming overly familiar with certain shots.

All players begin the game in D1, however, when a player loses two games in this division, they are demoted to D2. In order to get promoted from D2 you need to win two games in that division and so it goes on (i.e. if a player gets promoted and then loses another two games in D1, they are demoted again). The winner is the player who has the most points after a set time (e.g. 120 minutes) or when they reach a predetermined point total first. Games are played over four holes of stroke play and there is one simple rule manipulation that gives this game the extra dimension that needs to reach a stable level of performance quickly. That is, if a player goes two shots behind their opponent at any time the game is over and their opponent collects the points; 3 points are allocated for a win; 1 for a draw; 0 for a loss. Importantly, no points are gained for wins and draws in D2, in this division you are purely playing to get out of it. If matches are tied in D2, extra holes are played until a winner is established. Players play whoever is waiting around after other matches are finished.

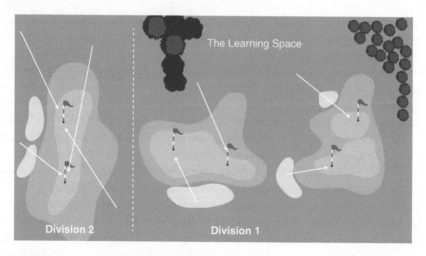

FIGURE 5.9 The set-up for the division 1 and 2 games.

In this activity, the scaling parameters of the playing space are further manipu-lated to heighten the need for good decision-making as well as controlling the golf ball's distance and direction. This is achieved by adding in boundaries and hazards using red cones as was illustrated earlier in Figure 5.1. The game is further enhanced by making 3 putts count as 4. A game could be lost on the first hole if, for example, Player A makes a 3 and Player B, on hitting the green in one shot precedes to 3-putt as this would mean they have carded a 5 on that hole. This game is designed to force the performer to recognise the demands of the task and what is required to perform well in it. In this sense the task 'invites' or 'constrains to afford' what needs to be learnt. A former national champion and current Scottish professional, on joining the group for the first time, reflecting on this game commented that,

> During this game I lost a lot of matches early on because I was too con-cerned about where not to hit it. I had to learn to focus on what I wanted to do, not what I didn't, then things really started to improve.

The learning that emerges out of this activity is different from player to player, for some, as the example above, it is a focus of attention issue; for others it is a rethink in terms of their strategic approach, and for others it is as straightforward as that they simply do not have the shots to deal with the performance problems that this game asks of them. The one piece of learning that can't be ignored, however, is that good performers in this task avoid penalty shots and 3-putts, they stabilise performance early and typically let inferior performers beat themselves. From time to time they will get a streak going of holed putts or make the odd bunker shot and, on these occasions, they win games quickly, but at all other times they are still willing to grind it out until these streaks come along. It worth reflecting at this point on the RLD of your session. Representative tasks and superior performers make excellent bed partners. If a known superior performer gets out-performed regularly by a known inferior performer, then the task probably doesn't recreate the real demands of tournament golf. This task passes the test with flying colours.

No 3 Putts

During the 2019 season, Nick Watney played 1,494 holes of golf and 3-putted 2.81% of them, making him the 100th best player on the PGA Tour for 3-putt avoidance. Leading the way for 3-putt avoidance in the same year was Wyndham Clark who 3-putted only 1.44% of the 1,530 holes he played meaning he had approximately one 3-putt for every four rounds of golf he played (https://www. pgatour.com/content/pgatour/stats/stat.426.y2019.html) – that's one 3-putt per 72 holes. Whilst 3-putt avoidance might imply a type of negative approach to the game, it should be noted that Clark had on average 4.21 (https://www.pgatour. com/players/player.51766.wyndham-clark.html) birdies every round ranking him as the 13th best player for this statistic. Whilst you could unpick the data further to tell a more complete story (i.e. Clark misses a lot of greens and ranked lowly overall in 2019 (https://www.pgatour.com/stats/stat.103.y2019.html), the fact remains that by any level analysis Tour players do not 3-putt very often.

The No 3 putt game is essentially a 3-putt avoidance game, but it is also a game that can only be completed if the players make a considerable number of 1-putts – and this is the beauty of the game. As previously mentioned, tour players make a high number of birdies but do so whilst hardly ever 3-putting. Not surprisingly then, Tour players make more par putts than they do birdie putts of the same distance ((Hunt, 2018) - implying a kind of risk aversion and the premium they put on par (see Chapter 1).

The game itself is very simple and the targets you set are dependent on the level of players you are working with. I set a target of getting to 10 under par on the basis that every hole is a par 2. The task is simple, a player needs to get to 10 under Par with no 3 putts and once they get to 10 under par they need to get through three more holes playing to par or under (the three additional holes replicates the conditions of being on the 'number' and then closing out the round). If they achieve this, the task is complete. However, if a player 3-putts at any point in this game, the player restarts the game on Level Par and goes again.

The set up for this game is simple and involves laying out a course on the putting green (I simply use tee-pegs to indicate where a player should start each hole from). We have nine holes available on our putting-green, so I set up three short putts (3–5 feet); three medium putts (8–12 feet), and 3 long putts (20 feet+). It is important that you change up the course on a regular basis to avoid the players getting familiar with lines and speed and to make the challenge more representative.

I remember when this activity was first introduced to one of my early HPTGs, or when a new group or player is introduced to it, the mood would start jovially with lots of laughing and joking, but before long the atmosphere would change and the noise levels become noticeably quieter. There are several attributes that appear to be fundamental to success in this task and I believe they are transferable to performance. Indeed, it is not uncommon to get feedback such as this from one of the groups:

> Its extremely beneficial, it pushes us and recreates the feelings we experience in tournament settings. I'd never really practiced in an environment that contains stress and pressure – and at the end of the day that's what we're trying to get better at.

These attributes include, patience and the ability to grind it out and the ability to make high pressure short putts for par over and over again, not to mention the resilience needed to start again after you have experienced a potentially demoralising 3-putt. When the members of group get to the level where they are regularly completing the task, I increase the intensity and demands of the challenge. I do this by introducing some shots from just off the green. This means that on at least one occasion they need to get up and down to stay in the game. For example, when a player has reached the required number and needs to close the activity out by getting through three further holes, I will make one of the holes a shot from off the green (but still a Par-2). The player now needs to get up and down in two to avoid undoing all the good work. The games detailed above are just snippets of the types of activities that I have found work over the years of working with many HPTGs. The activities and the manipulation of constraints, which by now you will recognise, are designed to destabilise the performers in such a way that is contextually relevant to their target performance level.

Conclusion

How successful you are at creating 'representative' training activities will reflect the extent to which you understand 'what' the demands are in relation to the level your players trying to get to. In an ideal scenario the structure of the training environment replicates exactly the structure of the performance environment. To this extent it is vitally important to get feedback from your performers to check how close you are to achieving this. In the early years of applying the CLA to the HPTG, it was clear I got many things wrong, often making challenges too difficult or tasks too complicated. I always say that if you need to clarify the rules of the 'game' after 30 minutes into it, then it's not a good game. A great 'game' can be explained quickly and simply and the feedback over the years has suggested that the sessions are achieving what they set out to achieve:

> The tasks are challenging, and they really create the pressures of tournament golf. This makes me really focused during training, I feel like I'm part of a culture of excellence.
>
> It's extremely beneficial, it pushes us and recreates the feelings we experience in tournament settings. I'd never really practiced in an environment

that contains stress and pressure – and at the end of the day that's what we're trying to get better at.

Another recurring theme of the feedback that I have received over the years is in relation to the motivation to practice:

> What I love about constraint training is that it makes practice more interesting and this type of training motivated me back to play golf again with more passion and made me enjoy it more in training because it challenged me.

I would like to finish this section by talking about a question I am often asked by other coaches. Because the HPTG environment is low-tech in nature, I get asked what I am measuring during training and what data I am collecting. My thoughts on the learning process can be put simply as I believe it to be 'the journey back from instability to stability'; I see it as my job to perturb the players (create instability) and then stand back and watch as they try to make the journey back to stability – the flexibility and speed at which they can do this is my measurement (although not quantifiable). How they do that will vary from performer to performer. What I do know however is that the more difficult it becomes to perturb or keep them perturbed, the more adapted they are becoming to the true demands of performance golf.

Key Points

- Solving the problem of hitting the ball well is easy, learning how to sustain a high-performance career is much more complex.
- HPTGs are a great way of training in a representative manner.
- If it doesn't look like and feel like the real thing then don't do it – you can't adapt to an environment you don't inhabit!
- Training should feel like it is harder than the real thing, suboptimal conditions are highly valued.
- Constraints are manipulated to deliberately destabilise the player in an attempt to induce adaptation in the mechanisms that control performance.
- Progress is measured by how difficult it is to destabilise the player.
- When destabilised, the speed at which the player can stabilise reflects the level of expertise in their performance 'system'.
- Training activities that are emotion-laden replicate the emotions of tournament golf
- Emotion-laden activities are end-directed in nature. The players strive towards achieving a task goal; the closer they get, the more emotional it becomes.
- Training sessions are unpredictable in nature, plans change, players should expect the unexpected.
- At the end of the day, mental and physical tiredness are a sign of a representative session.

6

EPILOGUE

Introduction

Our goal in this book was to create a landmark text for golf coaches and players in relation to applying a CLA to the player development process across the skill spectrum from beginners to elite. We have used case studies laced with practical examples from our work as professional golf coaches to demonstrate how we use a CLA to underpin our work with players with beginners, high-handicappers, aspirant tour players, and elite players already on the 'tour'. We wanted to bring the 'theory' to life and show how we apply the ideas in practice. To help achieve this goal and support any coach who is considering adopting a CLA, we conclude with the insights of Pete and Graeme about their own journey with CLA.

1. How Did You First Become Aware of CLA?

PETE: As part of my plan to change careers and become a professional golf coach, I decide to do a Masters course at University, and this is where I met Graeme. In my second year of study, he gave me the paper 'The Role of Ecological Constraints on Expertise Development' which was a paper all about how street football was the most instrumental factor in shaping top Brazilian footballer's early development. At the time I was reading every book I could on the golf swing, thinking that was the key to becoming a golf coach and the paper shifted my views considerably as it reminded me of how I and my peers developed as golfers. Obviously, this was not to the same level as the Brazilian footballers otherwise I would be retired on a beach in Malibu at the moment. After this, I immersed myself in the skill acquisition literature and also picked the brains of practitioners and began connecting with skill acquisition specialist across the world.

GRAEME: This isn't a straightforward question and as such this isn't a straight-forward answer because it was a gradual thing, and to some extent, I don't really remember. However, I do remember when the journey began as it was a journey that involved really reflecting on my own golf and my approach to coaching at the time. From a playing perspective, as a PGA Pro, I had turned professional with the intention of playing and put in thousands of hours into practising the game. My idol was Ben Hogan and I had read all about his legend in relation to the amount of practice he did – I followed that model, as did many others. Around the time I turned Pro, Nick Faldo was the best player in the world, and he had remodelled his swing and was known for hitting thousands of balls – this just validated my approach. So, following the 'champions model' of the day I spent most of my time tinkering with my swing spending hour upon hour on the range. The result was I became a good ball striker on the range but seldom could transfer it into good scores on the course. I'd practice all week and then get to a tournament and not be able to find that swing again, so I developed a 'tournament swing' that basically allowed me to keep the ball in play with a 'necky fade' and get it round in semi-respectable score – there was a lesson in that I just wasn't aware of it at the time.

When the playing didn't work out, I became a full-time coach and ba-sically just advocated that players do what I did, and also what I believed that the champions did, which was just work really hard, perfect the swing, and hit lots of balls. My coaching had become really stagnant, particularly when working with groups, and every session was similar to the last, that is, players in a line hitting balls, then some skill tests where players would see how many successful shots they could hit to a green from ten attempts or ladder-type putting drills. I was bored and not enjoying coaching, so I can only imagine what the players felt.

Looking to breathe new life into my coaching I enrolled in an MPhil at the University of Birmingham in 2006 and one of the lectures was on in-formation processing theory versus dynamical systems theory (DST). That's when I realised that what I was doing on the range was basically trying to program myself to be a better player by repeating what I believed was be-coming an optimal movement (I thought that's what Faldo and Hogan were doing). It never occurred to me that for this to work, essentially, I'd need to program hundreds of different movements, because no two shots are ever the same and never will I be able to retrieve them on demand.

Anyway, because my approach hadn't worked, I was keen to explore other explanations for skilled performance. Fortunately, through studying for my MPhil, suddenly, I had access to literature that I didn't know existed and I started to delve into DST. One of the first things I read was a book chapter called "Expert Performance in Sport: Views from the joint perspectives of Ecological Psychology and Dynamical Systems Theory," by Peter Beek and his colleagues; around the same time, I'd been reading some of the Teaching

Games for Understanding (TGfU) literature and putting some of that into practice. I felt there was something missing from the TGfU framework (but this could have been my lack of understanding) as it still seemed to have an emphasis on direct instruction but just couched within a game. It wasn't really until I read "Dynamics of skill acquisition: a constraints-led approach" that things started to click for me. It was like take the direct instruction bit out of TGfU and add in DST, and off we go – ha!

Ian's Comments

We can learn a lot about how we develop as coaches from the journeys of Graeme and Pete. First of all, they both displayed common traits that I have noticed when working with high-performing coaches; they were both proactive in developing their own knowledge and skills and were willing to invest time and money in that pursuit. Both have a thirst for knowledge and challenged their own thinking. Top coaches are always looking for an edge and are insatiable knowledge collectors. This is not always academic or research knowledge, and in fact we would argue that seeking out knowledge through experience, trying new things and speaking to other players and coaches can help bridge the gap in our knowledge (see Greenwood, Davids & Renshaw, 2014). However, they are also sceptical (in a positive way) and will challenge others to provide evidence to support new ideas. For me, this mindset is a pre-requisite to becoming the best coach you can be.

An interesting concept that underpins all coaches practice is their understanding of what it takes to become a good golfer, and what being a good golfer actually looks like. Pete highlights that when he read the article on the influence of playing in the street on the development of Brazilian foot footballers it reminded him of the way he learned to play golf with his peers. Undertaking unstructured practice has significant benefits, including the opportunities it provides to explore and develop creativity in solving problems. Additionally, the freedom to be autonomous in deciding what to practice promotes self-reliance and a capacity to take responsibility for one's own performance and development. Amisunderstanding often associated with unstructured play is that it lacks competitiveness, however, as Pete has revealed in his conversations, this environment was highly competitive and generally games were played for money. Hence, the ability to play 'under pressure' with 'high' stakes (which was highlighted by Graeme (Chapter 5)), was a constraint that Pete and his friends learned to deal with from an early age.

In contrast to Pete, Graeme spoke of the fact that most golfers base their understanding of how to practice – in order to become a good player – by observing older players, and the coaching that they receive. Basically, they work on the premise that "I am going to coach how I was coached, with that coach, coaching like he or she was coached" and so on. Essentially, the predominant belief is that technique is king and when a player does not perform to his/her own expectations there can be a tendency to go down the rabbit hole of changing technique (see Chapter 5). Added to that, the acquisition of the 'champions' swing is acquired through hours and hours of blocked practice on the range, often, focused on working on their weakest clubs. However, whilst hitting lots of balls is going to be better than not hitting any balls (maybe!), the 'return on your investment (of time)' is often much lower than one might expect. The 'quality' of practice is, therefore, more important than the 'quantity' of practice. One point I would make is that I believe that the standard interpretation of blocked practice from motor control is often not what golfers mean when they talk about it. This became clear to me after a long twitter exchange with a former golf coach a few months ago when we had a back and forward about the relative merits of blocked versus variable practice, and at the end when I asked him to describe blocked practice, he actually described variable practice! To clarify, motor control academics describe blocked practice as repeating the same movement from the same place over and over again. For example, hitting a 3 iron from the same bay, with the same flight to the same target when on the range. In contrast, variable practice would involve hitting the same club with different ball flights. Whilst many may think 'so what', we believe that when we discuss practice with coaches, we need a common understandable language to avoid confusion. As such, whatever the label, we would strongly support the second practice strategy as it encourages exploration and promotes adaptability, but would also suggest that if you're adding in different clubs (this would be described as random practice to replicate what actually takes place on the golf course) then that would be even better (see Chapter 4).

2. What Were the Key Things You Learned When You Began to Adopt CLA?

PETE: That it takes time and a level of expertise to develop understanding on how to create CLA learning environments. Sometimes the time aspect is not congruent with the commercial model of golf coaching. Get comfortable failing because you will fail a lot. Games that you have designed, planned, and excited about turn out to be massive flops, but then you as a coach need to learn and adapt from these experiences.

GRAEME: The biggest thing for me was the notion of manipulating constraints to change behaviour and to start to view the player as a dynamic system rather than a collection of isolated parts. It started to make sense to me that you could tell very little about how the golfer was going to perform by focusing on positions or parts of the swing. This resonated because as a golfer and coach I could make things look good but then the overall performance sometimes got worse. What followed was a large shift in my own thinking, away from thinking about what something looked like, towards placing a bigger emphasis being placed on how it performed – the term form follows function finally made sense to me. I learnt that CLA was a powerful framework for organising my thinking in relation to how to make good players better by manipulating the constraints impinging on them and RLD. It also became clear early on that working with the HPTG using a CLA, that there was a large shift in the players' motivation and enjoyment by comparison to my previously mentioned approach.

Ian's Comments

As highlighted by Pete and Graeme, just like becoming a good player, becoming a good coach requires a lot of time and effort and adopting new ideas can be challenging as initial attempts to run sessions may not be as effective as one might wish. For Graeme, this manifested itself in over-constraining sessions. These points highlight the importance of basing practice design on a clear understanding of learning, that is, by having a model of the learner and the learning process. An important point made by Graeme was his realisation that the golfer is a dynamic system where all parts of that system interact. Consequently, changing one part of the system causes a change to the whole system. When you accept this view of the golfer, the use of part learning, such as practising isolated parts of the swing to change performance, becomes pointless and leads to the use of constraints to shape (or promote self-organisation) of performance. In the book, we have provided many examples, but the important point here is that the constraint needs to be designed-in based on an understanding of the principles of CLA. Adding in constraints because it is what the approach says we should do without understanding the possible impact on performance or over-constraining which can act to prescribe the solution rather than allow the golfer to find the right solution is a common issue for those new to CLA. Knowing how a constraint is going to impact the individual golfer (some constraints work for all golfers whilst some may only work with one) can sometimes be a leap into the unknown, but rather than shy away from trying, I would encourage coaches to simply have a go at it and then carefully monitor the impact. Once the impact has been assessed, then the constraint or the task can be tweaked. I like the concept of iterations adopted by inventors and designers, they start with the 'best' version they can come up with at the time and then simply test it and keep modifying until they come up with better and better solutions. In summary, exploration to search for the most functional solution is just as much a part of learning to coach as is it is to play.

3. What Were the Key Challenges?

PETE: Managing players expectations. Many golfers have been brought up on the staple diet of "if you perform poorly it is the golf swing, so fix the golf swing". Therefore, a lot of time spent educating golfers on the reasoning why exploration and adaptation in coaching sessions is important. Also, working over the winter in an indoor simulator (due to weather and light), challenged my early readings on representative learning environments

(I thought all coaching needed to be in context). However, in practice, some of the players I have helped in the indoor areas got considerably better without me ever seeing them playing golf. Therefore, for some golfers, helping to build awareness of what the tool (i.e., the club) can do and how it can be manipulated when striking a golf ball can have considerable benefits.

GRAEME: The key challenge was changing people's mindset towards the role of practice and the way they practice. Golfers who do practice, and a lot don't, almost always don't practice in the field of play. Instead, they will go to a range or a short game area and typically use block practice (i.e. hit ball after ball). That is not to say there isn't a time and place for this, but I don't feel it should be where you spend most of your practice time. I would ask any player this; how often have you hit the ball well at the range and then when you went on to the course you played badly? How often have you hit it badly at the range and then played well on the course? These are key questions because we can all relate to them and we've all experienced poor transfer of our practice to the golf course. You ultimately know it's not working when you're working hard (it's easy to work hard) but you're not getting better and some cases getting worse.

Another key challenge to getting people to adopt a CLA as the main part of their development is that progress can be perceived to be slower than that of a more traditional approach. Traditionally, if you go for a lesson on a driving range to improve your driving you will probably see an immediate improvement – particularly if the coach has launch monitor data where, for example, you might see your clubhead speed has gone up, spin rate has come down, and you're carry distance is further. So, traditionally, learning is viewed as linear in golf, with the improvement proportional to what you went to work on. The problem is your driving data on the range may be improving whilst your scores on the golf course may not be, this is sometimes written off as a performer error, that is, the player knows what to do but they're not doing it.

In contrast, improvement using the CLA is a little messier than this and you can't always predict what the player is going to learn or put a timescale on it. This is because there's no direct instruction, instead, I like to create contextually relevant problems and challenge the player to find a solution. Not everyone likes this, and some prefer just to be told what to do – even if this approach hasn't worked for them in the past.

Ian's Comments: Changing the mindset of coaches and particularly players who have been brought up on the standard narrative that you can only become good by spending hours and hours on the range is once again a common problem across sports. An early 'win' or success is often the key to acceptance of the ideas and the coach needs to be 'canny' in deciding what to initially work on with a player. A good example was how Pete worked with John in the golf chapter in the foundation book. The almost 'instant' success of the coaching session to help John learn to draw his driver showed how important it is to get to know the player before implementing the intervention, a point emphasised strongly in this book (Chapter 2). The advantages of a CLA to actual performance in competition ON the course become clear fairly quickly as highlighted by Graeme, which can be a little counter-intuitive, as training is much messier than traditional coaching and hence practising using a CLA can appear to be having little impact or even feel as though it is having a negative effect.

Pete's reflection on the positive impact of working indoors on trackman deserves some comment. The concept of RLD has been taken by some to mean that all practice must take place in the performance environment, however, we have attempted to refute this idea by developing the 'representativeness' dial. This dial encourages the coach to consider how much the practice session 'looks and feels like the real thing', and highlights that any activity that breaks up the skill should be bracketed in the 'red zone' and should be avoided if possible. An interesting idea is how to rate simulators and virtual reality training in terms of its representativeness. Given the potential to create similar emotions and thoughts when immersed in virtual environments as seen in 'real' situations, a golf simulator is potentially an exciting tool for golfers and in the field of sport psychology and motor learning warrants further research to explore its strengths and weaknesses. Additionally, the value of using imagery to enhance performance is well known and coaches may well find value in looking at combining simulators and imagery as part of training programmes, especially during off-season periods where the course is inaccessible.

4. What Were Some of the Typical Mistakes That You Made?

PETE: Early on, my understanding of a CLA approach was lacking. I believed that it was fully hands-off coaching, so developed a laissez faire approach, before later reflecting that some players needed more help and that may include technical help, such as helping someone to change the way they hold a golf club. Also, with better players I stretched them too much with really hard task constraints, causing some conflict, loss of trust, and motivation. So, finding the optimal stretch in a session, as the years go on, I can spot when a session isn't working fairly quickly and I am not afraid to change it up when previously I would be scared to change it and probably didn't have enough strings to my bow to be able to mix it up anyway.

GRAEME: For me, in the early days, it was manipulating the task conditions too much and players still having to ask what the constraints are well into the task; the other thing was just making the task rules too difficult and players would become really demotivated because they could see early on that the task couldn't be completed successfully. A great constraints session is all about simplicity of design that allows clarity and brevity of explanation.

Also, you need to assess the readiness of some players to train in this way, particularly if they are used to fairly controlled and predictable training methods. I didn't give enough thought to this and just threw everyone straight into it. CLA sessions can get really tense, they're emotional and players need to be ready for this – I didn't give enough thought to this in the early days. I remember one player saying that CLA sessions had made him realise that he didn't have what it took to play high-level golf, that he couldn't handle the intensity or pressure. He felt that I brought forward something that he would have found out later; in a sense, he felt it was better to know sooner. When he told me this, I realised I was getting something wrong!

Ian's Comments

Pete describes initially adopting a fully hands-off, laissez faire coaching approach where he designed-in task constraints and then simply left the player(s) to fend for themselves. Again, this is a common misconception about CLA, and whilst the approach is certainly more hands-off than traditional approaches, it is not hands-free. Coaching using a CLA requires the ability to carefully observe the impact of the constraints and then work out what to change or what to say to support learning. Sometimes this might mean making the task easier or harder, providing hints or asking questions to encourage the player to search in specific areas for the answer. An important point is that the whole session should not push the player to his limits, and as highlighted by Pete and Graeme, careful attention needs to be made to make sure the task difficulty allows some level of success during the session. Motivation levels of players can be closely connected to the perception of the challenge and coaches need to check engagement throughout the session. Of course, this does not mean that if a player becomes frustrated due to failure that the coach should always simply modify the task to make it easier, but rather should carefully consider if there is anything he or she can say to support the player in these situations. Coaches need to be aware that when a player is struggling to learn something new it is likely to lead to an increase in intensity and range of emotions. The coach needs to be ready for this and have the right words cued up, ready to provide support which may be as simple as reminding them that their emotions are normal and expected when learning something new or directing search towards the key areas of the movement upon which to focus. It is also worth reminding them that these are the types of feelings that they will have to learn to deal with in the competition. One final point, when a movement such as a golf swing involves using the whole body, knowing which part of the body to invite players to focus upon can be very challenging. One strategy is for coaches to ask questions that develop self-awareness through analogies or metaphors that capture the whole movement (see Chapter 4).

5. What Has Surprised You About Using a CLA?

PETE: How much planning is needed. Sometimes all/most of the work is done before the session with small interventions during the session.

GRAEME: The biggest surprise of all of this is more to do with the players and especially young players. And I do think it's a generational thing. I talked earlier about using perturbations to destabilise players and I am often surprised how easy it to do this with players who have low handicaps and aspirations to play at a high level. I think because many have been so conditioned to block practising, using launch monitors and videoing their swings that they lack a bit of creativity. With my approach to applying the CLA, there's a lot of variability built in; no two shots or situations are the same. I remember once setting up a situation where a bunker shot had to played from the back of a bunker, where, in order to play it they needed to stand with one foot in and one foot out of the bunker and use a steep angle of attack – I was amazed at the difficulty the group had in playing this shot. One player said he'd never had to play a shot like this before, which amazed me. The good thing after training with a CLA approach for a while was that the player does become more adaptable. I often observe members of the HPTG during tournaments and whenever they play a good shot from a tricky spot, they'll typically turn to me and say that's the 'constraint' training. Interestingly, for me, this was exactly what we did when I was younger when we were practising. This is captured well by a former member of the HPTG:

> I started constraints training about 5 months ago (2017) and I've played in a couple of tournaments and a couple of rounds of golf under pressure that I have to perform and I've had a couple of tricky shots out there on the course and I'm thinking well you've done this before, you've done this shot before …this is what you do this training for, the constraints led practice, because in constraints led training you're under pressure against highly skilled professionals or elite amateurs…when you feel…you're stuck behind a bunker on a golf course you feel well it's no problem and you've got a variety of shots on the course you can play to help you succeed.

Ian's Comments

Pete's comments about the amount of planning required to coach using a CLA is a good one and the sheer weight of concepts to consider can initially feel overwhelming. However, we were aware of these issues and put together this book series to try and help coaches new to CLA. The tools we introduced in the Foundation book in the 'Building a Bridge' section of the book provide a template for designing CLA sessions and provide resources including the Constraints Builder, the Environment Selector, and a Session Planning template. Specifically, for the golf coach, these tools are brought to life in the golf chapter and provide a clear step-by-step road map for planning and running CLA sessions.

Graeme's comments once again highlight how different CLA is in terms of the response of players who are new to the ideas. CLA really changes the way that players learn and acceptance of the thoughts and emotions that come with this is a key stage in buying into the process. For coaches, it is worth checking on players in terms of their ABCs: Affect (how they are feeling); Behaviour (how they are acting); Cognitions (what they are thinking). A good prompt would be to ask players to compare their ABCs at critical moments in competitions and how the practice tasks and session are making them feel. Making players more comfortable with practising whilst having similar thoughts and feelings as they solve game-like problems is a powerful outcome, and as highlighted by the players coached by Graeme, it can enhance confidence when competing.

6. How Do Your Players React to This New Approach?

PETE: In the main very well because using a CLA approach when done right increases enjoyment/engagement in a coaching session and players report back that it looks, smells, and feels more like golf.

GRAEME: Above all the reaction of the players have really fuelled this for me. Apart from anything, students are really motivated to train, and to do more, when it's a CLA session. For players who are coming in new to an HPTG, they've almost always never trained like this before. That can be difficult because the ones who have been in the HPTG for the longest are more adapted to the conditions of the CLA and new players coming in can find it difficult at first. However, the easiest way to answer the question, is to share two of the themes (motivation and emotions) in relation to 'players reaction to this approach' that have emerged from talking to players:

Motivation

I would tend to get a little bit bored at the driving range because you're standing in the one spot all the time and you're hitting from the one spot but in the CLA you're always moving around, you're off grass and it's also more competitive and fun, I like competitive practice, obviously on course you want to win and during the CLA you want to win and that is a big thing I enjoy about it.

It had been eight years of doing constant practice the same drills. it was too boring. I didn't see improvement, that was making me upset. When I went to the CLA I had to put more effort in as it was more difficult. Then I saw a difference when I went to play and I found this fascinating and felt motivated to do more.

What I love about constraint training is that it makes practice more interesting and this type of training motivated me back to play golf again with more passion and made me enjoy it more in training because it challenged me.

Emotions

Well it puts you under pressure puts you in a game like situation, you can relate to the emotions from the practice to the golf course. It's emotional.

It helps you emotionally. You always go up and down. Like if you duff a chip...you could do that in real life as well...you need to adapt to that...and also adapt to the shot emotionally and...you're never hitting the same shot twice.

Ian's Comments

In our previous work (Renshaw et al., 2012; Chow et al., 2015) we have highlighted that one of the strengths of a CLA is that if designed correctly it can meet the basic psychological needs of individual learners. In line with self-determination theory, CLA coaching that ensures that learners can demonstrate competence, have autonomy over what they choose to do, and how to do it and have a sense of relatedness to their coach then it is more likely they will develop a greater level of intrinsic or self-determined motivation. Of course, achieving these goals requires careful planning and a good understanding of the player's ability and personality type especially in early CLA sessions if a player is new to the approach. A good strategy would be to introduce the ideas slowly and gradually move to a complete CLA.

7. What Advice Would You Give to Coaches (or Players) Thinking of Adopting a CLA in Their Own Practice?

PETE: Go in with an open mind, don't be scared to try new things. For coaches, Graeme and I in the early years developed a test group to try new ideas and get feedback from the players on the CLA sessions. Invaluable learning for Graeme and I. For players, try and use some of the principles gleaned from this book or get in touch, we are more than happy to talk through any questions you have when trying to implement this approach to your own golf.

GRAEME: Hopefully by this stage in the book, you are familiar enough with the CLA and the theory behind it to be able to articulate what problem the CLA is trying to solve. Your ability to do this concisely will be fundamental to getting buy-in from players. When it comes to running sessions, remember the earlier advice that if it doesn't look like or feel like the real thing then don't do it – if it is recognisable to the real game and it challenges them fairly then you'll get an emotional and motivational reaction from the players. Lastly, and as previously mentioned, simplicity is key when it comes to session design, don't add in extra rules just to make a task more difficult as that can be counterproductive and demotivating to a player.

If you're a player, I'd recommend hooking up with a coach who is familiar with the CLA and try to get a training group started. The group scenario is ideal because you have people to compete against. Putting on CLA training days can also be a good way to build interest and also be a good earner for a coach while inexpensive for each player. For players, if you can't get a group together, then actively seek out players who are better than you and play with them, be that in the club medal or competitions out with your club, play harder courses and play different types of courses as often as you can, that is inland, links etc – if you do that you will be applying the CLA to your own game.

Ian's Comments

Graeme and Pete's use of cooperative 'test groups' is a great idea when trying new ideas in CLA and making the players feel part of the process is important to ensure that you get honest feedback on sessions. Another idea I would strongly support is connecting with other coaches who are implementing CLA in their coaching and they do not necessarily have to be golf coaches, as often much can be learned from coaches who can see issues from an alternative perspective (unconditioned to 'golf thinking'). Developing practice squads is also a great idea as it enables you to build the culture of competition through cooperation from which many top golfers have emerged. If this is difficult, Graeme's suggestion of working with other coaching groups is also a good one, especially as new interactions can enhance cross-fertilisation of ideas and keep players 'fresh', which can be a problem when playing with or against the same players every session. My final point is to reiterate Graeme's key point; keep it simple and 'don't add in in extra rules just to make a task more difficult as that can be counterproductive and demotivating to a player.'

8. Any Final Comments?

PETE: Reflecting and as my experience grows as a coach, I am always drawn to a paper that Graeme passed over a few years ago, that of a bricoleur coach (Bush & Silk, 2010):

"The distinguishing feature of a bricoleur is the ability to make do with materials and tools which are at hand (Weick, 1985) in response to what happens. In contrast to an engineer, who will seek to define what happens with more predictability, the bricoleur adopts the rule to 'always make do with what's available" (Levi-Strauss, 1962, p. 31). For the coach as bricoleur, who may well have undertaken training in particular models or assessed skills against a competence framework, such tools are not used as the sole means for working in the coaching encounter, instead, such tools are added to a variety of others in the form of past experiences, skills, and understandings which may or may not be related to coaching. The point is the ability to adjust their use for a particular moment (Louridas, 1996).'

It's one I continually strive to be.

GRAEME: As mentioned above its worthwhile looking at putting training groups together as this can work really well, and I'd also encourage collaboration with other coaches in terms of putting players together for sessions. This is in the players' best interests, as the more good players they play with the better they will be playing with unfamiliar people in the future. The last thing I would say is when applying the CLA is to try different things and experiment. The players will soon let you know how good your ideas are.

Ian's Final Comments

In summary, throughout the book, we have provided a wide range of practical examples of how we implement a CLA in our golf coaching. There are a few points we believe is worth reinforcing. First, when adopting a CLA in golf coaching every activity needs to have a defined intention which requires the coach to ensure that the key affordances that provide opportunities to shape perception-action skills are present in the practice environment. Designing-in affordances to practice is closely tied to the concept of representative design; considering if the practice task looks and feels as close as possible to the real thing ensures that there is a good transfer from practice to performance. Defining purpose and consequences in session design is essential to RLD. When considering the constraints that coaches add into practice, they should ensure that they link to the session intentions. Learning how to manipulate constraints is a key skill for practitioners who wish to implement a CLA and there is plenty of anecdotal evidence that golf coaches have intuitively been able to identify and manipulate the key constraints acting on learners (Renshaw et al., 2010). However, the key to a successful application of a CLA is dependent on an understanding of the key processes that take place when constraints change due to uncontrolled factors (e.g., changes in the weather) or are deliberately manipulated by practitioners (e.g., changing task constraints or creating higher levels of emotion). Consequently, ensuring that constraints are manipulated in a principled manner is essential to prevent over-constraining or providing inappropriate tasks. Essential to the effective implementation of constraints is understanding how the constraint acts to invite attunement to the key affordances of the environment. Finally, the level of repetition without repetition should ensure that the amount of variability built into practice is matched to the current needs of the player.

We hope you enjoyed this book and that it has offered you an insight into how golf coaches can implement CLA in their work. If you are new to the ideas of CLA, we hope that we have captured your interest enough to give it a go. Just like learning to play golf, exploration is a key to improvement when implementing CLA in golf coaching. Of course, as we chose to demonstrate the ideas across all levels from beginner through to elite golfer, at times we feel as though we have only scratched the surface. For us, the journey has only just begun and we are excited to see where, with your help, we can improve CLA coaching in golf and help give our golfers of whatever level, an enjoyable learning experience that enables them to become as hooked on to the game as we are.

REFERENCES

Albright, C. R. (2017). Does the effect of driving distance on PGA/LPGA tour earnings differ across genders? *20th Annual Georgia College Student Research Conference*. https://kb.gcsu.edu/src/2017/friday/16.

Araújo, D., Fonseca, C., Davids, K. W., Garganta, J., Volossovitch, A., Brandão, R., & Krebs, R. (2010). The role of ecological constraints on expertise development. *Talent Development & Excellence*, 2(2), 165–179.

Araújo, D. & Davids, K. (2011). What exactly is *acquired* during skill acquisition? *Journal of Consciousness Studies*, 18, 7–23.

Arnott, P. (2019). *Scottish European tour professionals experiences of playing and developing towards the European tour: Through the lens of a constraints-led approach* https://rke.abertay.ac.uk/en/studentTheses/scottish-european-tour-professionals-experiences-of-playing-and-d.

Ballesteros, S. (2007). *Seve: The official biography*. London: Yellow Jersey Press.

Bernstein, N. A. (1967). *The co-ordination and regulation of movements: Conclusions towards the study of motor co-ordination*. Biodynamics of Locomotion, 104–113.

Broadie, M. (2014). *Every shot counts: Using the revolutionary strokes gained approach to improve your golf performance and strategy*. New York: Gotham Books.

Bull, M. (2015). *Range vs course – How do players move?* Retrieved 1st March 2020 from http://bull3d.co.uk/Bull3DSocial/file/view/983/range-vs-course-how-do-players-move.

Bush, A. & Silk, M. (2010). Towards an evolving critical consciousness in coaching research: The physical pedagogic bricolage. *International Journal of Sports Science & Coaching*, 5(4), 551–565.

Button, C., Seifert, L., Chow, J. Y., Davids, K. & Araujo, D. (2020). *Dynamics of skill acquisition: An ecological dynamics approach*. Champaign, IL: Human Kinetics Publishers.

Carello, C., Thuot, S. & Turvey, M. T. (2000). Aging and the perception of a racket's sweet spot. *Human Movement Science*, 19, 1–20.

Clark, R. (2014). *Phil Scott is the man behind the man in the green jacket, here are his tips to raising a champion*. Australian Golf Digest. Retrieved 1st March 2020 from https://www.theaustralian.com.au/sport/phil-scott-is-the-man-behind-the-man-in-the-green-jacket-here-are-his-tips-to-raising-a-champ/news-story/f6dd0d3552d3de4774ad74db37c1d776.

Clark, R. D. (2005). An analysis of players' consistency among professional golfers: A longitudinal study. *Perceptual and Motor Skills*, 101(2), 365–372. doi:10.2466/pms.101.2.365–372.

Chemero, A. (2003). An outline of a theory of affordances. *Ecological Psychology*, 15, 181–195. doi:10.1207/S15326969ECO1502_5.

Chow, J. Y., Davids, K., Button, C. & Renshaw, I. (2015). *Nonlinear pedagogy in skill acquisition: An introduction*. London: Routledge.

Chow, J. Y., Davids, K., Button, C., Shuttleworth, R., Renshaw, I. & Araujo, D. (2006). Nonlinear pedagogy: A constraints-led framework for understanding emergence of game play and movement skills. *Nonlinear Dynamics, Psychology, and Life Sciences*, 10(1), 71–103.

Crowe, C. (2016). What has gone wrong at the Home of Golf? With no young Scots on any major tour, the country that invented the game is in crisis. *Scottish Daily Mail*, 8th January 2016. Retrieved 4th March 2020 from Scottish Daily Mail. 8/1/2016 (https://www.dailymail.co.uk/sport/golf/article-3388982/What-gone-wrong-Home-Golf-no-young-Scots-major-tour-country-invented-game-crisis.html.)

Curtner-Smith, M. D., Todorovich, J. R., McCaughtry, N. A. & Lacon, S. A. (2001). Urban teachers use of productive and reproductive teaching styles within the confines of the national curriculum for physical education. *European Physical Education Review*, 7(2), 177–190.

Davids, K. W., Button, C. & Bennett, S. J. (2008). *Dynamics of skill acquisition: A constraints-led approach*. Champaign, IL: Human Kinetics.

Edelman, G. M. & Gally, J. A. (2001). Degeneracy and complexity in biological systems. *Proceedings of the National Academy of Sciences*, 98(24), 13763–13768.

Evans, K. & Tuttle, N. (2015). Improving performance in golf: Current research and implications from a clinical perspective. *Brazilian Journal of Physical Therapy*, 19(5), 381–389.

Faldo, N. (2019). *Nick Faldo have some armour*. Retrieved 4th March 2020 from https://vimeo.com/298738733.

Fawcett, S. (2019). Personal communication to Graeme McDowell. email correspondence. 6/11/2019.

Fine, L. (2015). Spieth says he won Tour Championship with his head. *Reuters*, 28th September 2015. Retrieved 4th March 2020 from https://www.reuters.com/article/golf-pga-spieth-idINKCN0RS07L20150928.

Gallwey, W. T. (1979). *The inner game of golf*. London: Jonathan Cape.

Gibson, J. J. (1986). *The ecological approach to visual perception*. New York: Psychology Press.

Greenwood, D., Davids, K., & Renshaw, I. (2014). Experiential knowledge of expert coaches can help identify informational constraints on performance of dynamic interceptive actions. *Journal of Sports Sciences*, 32(4), 328–335.

Headrick, J., Renshaw, I., Davids, K., Pinder, R. A. & Araújo, D. (2015). The dynamics of expertise acquisition in sport: The role of affective learning design. *Psychology of Sport and Exercise*, 16, 83–90.

Hunt, R. (2018). *Pro golf synopsis. The indispensable handbook to the 2018 golf season*. Retrieved 4th March 2020 from progolfsynopsis@yahoo.com.

Jenkins, S. (2014). Professionalism, golf coaching and a Master of Science degree. *International Journal of Sports Science & Coaching*, 9(4), 693–715.

Kahneman, D. (2011). *Thinking, fast and slow* (Kindle Edition). New York: Farrar, Straus and Giroux.

Kelso, J. S. (1995). *Dynamic patterns: The self-organization of brain and behavior*. Cambridge: MIT press.

Koepka, B. (2019). The player's championship. Retrieved 1st March 2020 from http://www.asapsports.com/show_interview.php?id=147685.

Keogh, J. W. & Hume, P. A. (2012). Evidence for biomechanics and motor learning research improving golf performance. *Sports Biomechanics*, 11(2), 288–309.

Khan, C. H. (2003). *The art and thoughts of Heraclitus: An edition of the fragments with translation and commentary.* Cambridge: Cambridge University press.

Kiverstein, J. & Rietveld, E. (2015). The primacy of skilled intentionality: On Hutto & Satne's the natural origins of content. *Philosophia*, 43(3), 701–721.

Levi-Strauss, C. (1962). *La Pensee Sauvage.* Paris: Librairie Plon.

Louridas, P. (1996). Design a bricolage: Anthropology meets design thinking. *Design Studies*, 20(6), 517–535.

MacAuley, C. (2020). *T-14th at the Columbia Championship.* Retrieved 4th March 2020 from http://www.callummacaulaygolf.com/latest-scores/t-14th-at-the-columbia-championship/#more-129.

McDowall, G. (2011). *The problem with Stack and tilt.* Retrieved 4th March 2020 from http://sportsexpertise.blogspot.com/2011/08/problem-with-stack-and-tilt.html.

Montero, Toner & Moran, (2019). Questioning the breadth of the attentional focus effect. In. M. L. Cappuccio (ed.). *Handbook of embodied cognition and sport psychology* (pp. 199–222). Cambridge: MIT Press:

Murray, E. (2018). *Decade elapses since Tiger Woods won his last major – On one leg.* Retrieved 4th March 2020 from www.theguardian.com/sport/2018/jun/11/decade-elapses-tiger-woods-last-major-one-leg-golf.

Newell, K. M., & Ranganathan, R. (2010). Instructions as constraints in motor skill acquisition. In I. Renshaw, K.D. Davids & G. Savelebergh (eds.). *Motor learning in practice* (pp. 37–52). London: Routledge.

PGA Tour (2019). *Tiger Woods' first interview after Masters victory No. 5.* Retrieved 1st March 2020 from https://www.youtube.com/watch?v=pvxJP0TIXGo.

Player, G. *In conversation with world renowned golf coach Cameron McCormick.* Retrieved 4th March 2020 from https://podcasts.apple.com/za/podcast/mastery-mindset-ep-045/id1389067304?i=1000449462647.

Renshaw, I., Davids, K., Araújo, D., Lucas, A. & Roberts, W. M. (2019). Understanding the merits of 'brain-training' in sport: How perception, cognition and action underpins performance. *Frontiers in Psychology.* doi:10.3389/fpsyg.2018.02468.

Renshaw, I., Davids, K., Chow, J. & Hammond, J. (2010). A constraints-led perspective to understanding skill acquisition and game play: A basis for integration of motor learning theory and physical education praxis? *Physical Education and Sport Pedagogy*, 15(2), 117–131.

Renshaw, I., Davids, K., Newcombe, D. & Roberts, W. (2019). *The constraints-led approach: Principles for sports coaching and practice design.* London: Routledge.

Renshaw, I. & Moy, B. (2018). A constraint-led approach to coaching and teaching games: Can going back to the future solve the "they need the basics before they can play a game" argument? *Ágora para la Educación Física y el Deporte*, 20, 1–26.

Renshaw, I., Oldham, A. R. & Bawden, M. (2012). Nonlinear pedagogy underpins intrinsic motivation in sports coaching. *The Open Sports Sciences Journal*, 5, 88–99.

Rietveld, E. & Kiverstein, J. (2014). A rich landscape of affordances. *Ecological Psychology*, 26(4), 325–352.

Rochat, N., Seifert, L., Guignard, B. & Hauw, D. (2019). An enactive approach to appropriation in the instrumented activity of trail running. *Cognitive Processing*, 20(4), 459–477.

Schmidt, R. A. & Lee, T. D. (2013). *Motor learning and performance: From principles to application.* Champaign, IL: Human Kinetics.

Scott, P. *Interview.* Retrieved 4th March 2020 from http://www.theaustralian.com.au/sport/phil-scott-is-the-man-behind-the-man-in-the-green-jacket-here-are-his-tips-to-raising-a-champ/news-story/f6dd0d3552d3de4774ad74db37c1d776.

Seve Ballesteros Foundation. *Biography.* Retrieved 4th March 2020 from https://seveballesteros.com/en/seve/biography/.

Rochat, N., Seifert, L., Guignard, B., & Hauw, D. (2019). An enactive approach to appropriation in the instrumented activity of trail running. *Cognitive Processing,* 20(4), 459–477.

Fine, L. (2015). Spieth says he won Tour Championship with his head. *Reuters,* 28th September 2015. Retrieved 4th March 2020 from https://www.reuters.com/article/golf-pga-spieth-idINKCN0RS07L20150928

Tan, C. W. K., Chow, J. Y. & Davids, K. (2012). 'How does TGfU work?': Examining the relationship between learning design in TGfU and a nonlinear pedagogy. *Physical Education and Sport Pedagogy,* 17(4), 331–348.

Tancredi. (n.d.). *Talk: The leopard.* Retrieved 4th March 2020 from https://en.wikipedia.org/wiki/Talk%3AThe_Leopard.

Thelen, E. & Smith, L. B. (1996). *A dynamic systems approach to the development of cognition and action.* Cambridge: MIT press.

Vuchi, F. (2014). *Tiger woods: Swing coaches can't know what players feel.* Retrieved 4th March 2020 from https://www.golf.com/tour-and-news/tiger-woods-swing-coaches-cant-know-what-players-feel.

Warren, W. H. & Verbrugge, R. R. (1984). Auditory perception of breaking and bouncing events: A case study in ecological acoustics. *Journal of Experimental Psychology: Human Perception and Performance,* 10(5), 704.

Weick, K. E. (1985). Systematic observational methods. In. G. Lindzey & E. Aronson (Eds.). *The handbook of social psychology* (pp. 567–634). London: Wiley.

Wittgenstein, L. (1953). *Philosophical investigations.* Oxford, UK: Blackwell.

Withagen, R., Araújo, D. & de Poel, H. J. (2017). Inviting affordances and agency. *New Ideas in Psychology,* 45, 11–18.

Withagen, R., De Poel, H. J., Araújo, D. & Pepping, G. J. (2012). Affordances can invite behavior: Reconsidering the relationship between affordances and agency. *New Ideas in Psychology,* 30(2), 250–258.

Woods, E. & McDaniel, P. (1997). Training a tiger: A father's guide to raising a winner in golf and life. New York: HarperCollins.

Woods, T. (2017). *Tiger's pProwl.* Retrieved 4th March 2020 from https://www.youtube.com/watch?v=2fnHJuUGm5A.

Woolly, D. (2014). *Paidrig Harrington: I grew up gambling on golf.* https://www.independent.ie/sport/golf/padraig-harrington-i-grew-up-gambling-on-golf-30702427.html.

Wulf, G. (2013). Attentional focus and motor learning: A review of 15 years. *International Review of Sport and Exercise Psychology,* 6(1), 77–104.

INDEX

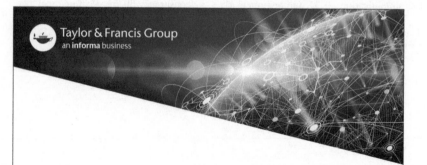